# TRIBAL MOVEMENTS IN JHARKHAND 1857-2007

## About the Editors

**Asha Mishra,** an alumnus of Bhagalpur University, has been teaching History since 1977. She is presently the Reader and Head of the Department, Mahila College, Chaibasa. She was awarded Ph.D. degree in 1984 by the Bhagalpur University on the Political History of Nepal during 1804-1846. She is presently engaged in research on the tribal history of Singhbhum.

**Chittaranjan Kumar Paty,** an alumnus of Ranchi University, has retired as Reader and Head, Department of History, Tata College, Chaibasa. He was awarded Ph.D. degree in 1991 by Ranchi University. Besides contributing research papers to different journals, he has published *History of Seraikela and Kharsawan States* (2002) and *Forest, Government and Tribe* (ed.) (2007). Presently, he is working on the history of Jharkhand.

# TRIBAL MOVEMENTS
# IN
# JHARKHAND 1857-2007

*Edited by*
Asha Mishra
Chittaranjan Kumar Paty

CONCEPT PUBLISHING COMPANY PVT. LTD.
NEW DELHI-110 059

**ISBN-13: 978-81-8069-686-2**

First Published 2010

*Published and Printed by*

**Concept Publishing Company Pvt. Ltd.**
**Regd. Office :**
A/15-16, Commercial Block, Mohan Garden
New Delhi-110059 (India)
*Phones* : 25351460, 25351794, *Fax* : 091-11-25357109
*Email* : publishing@conceptpub.com
*Website*: www.conceptpub.com

**Editorial Office :**
H-13, Bali Nagar, New Delhi-110 015, India.

Cataloging in Publication Data-- *Courtesy:* D.K. Agencies (P) Ltd. <docinfo@dkagencies.com>

**Tribal movements in Jharkhand, 1857-2007** / edited by Asha Mishra, Chittaranjan Kumar Paty.
p. cm.
Papers presented at a national conference held at Chaibasa during 7-8 March 2008.
Includes bibliographical references.
Includes index.
ISBN 13: 9788180696862 ISBN 10 8180696863

1. Jharkhand (India)--Scheduled tribes--Politics and government--Congresses. 2. Social movements--India--Jharkhand--History--Congresses. 3. Peasant uprisings--India--Jharkhand--History--Congresses. 4. Jharkhand (India)--Politics and government--Congresses. I. Mishra, Asha. II. Paty, Chittaranjan Kumar, 1946-

DDC 305.5680954127 22

# Preface

The chapters in this book had been contributed to the National Conference organized by the Department of History, Mahila College, Chaibasa on 7-8 March, 2008 which was sponsored by the UGC, Eastern Regional Office, Kolkata. The theme of the conference was Indigenous Movements in Jharkhand (1857-2007).

The State of Jharkhand is surrounded by thick jungles and the Singhbhum region is predominantly inhabited by the tribals. The tribal movements which had occurred in this area often asserted land, water and forest centric identity. Thus the theme of the Conference took shape. It was divided into three sub-parts (1) Revolt of 1857-58 and the indigenes; (2) assertion of identity over *Jal, Jungle* and *Jameen* 1858-2007; and (3) cultural identity and the *Adivasis*.

The essays included in this volume emphasized ideas and issues relevant for a closer understanding of the indigenous movements. A.K. Sen explores the role of Gono Pingua, a tribal leader of South Kolhan whom mainstream historiography had not till recently been able to foreground. Examining different sources he highlights the work of Gono Pingua both as an associate of Raja Arjun Singh of Porahat and a leader of ethnic upsurge during the Revolt of 1857. The essay thus succeeds in fleshing out the momentous *adivasi* anti-British struggle and conducts the epistemic rebirth of a regional tribal leader from oblivion.

The heroic role of Nilambar and Pitamber of Palamau is the theme of the essay by I.K. Choudhary. He explains the different causes which led to the Revolt of 1857 in Palamau under their leadership. The rebels had the support of the people of Palamu who were able to forge a link with the insurgents of

Ranchi, Hazaribagh, Singhbhum Mirzapur including Amar Singh and Babu Kunwar Singh. Both leaders fought against British rule but lastly they were captured and executed by the British, which put an end to the movement. The author has been able to highlight that uprising marked by a unique combination of subaltern and feudal forces of the area.

That since the ancient times to the Jharkhand movement the tribals have always been subjected to oppression by the outsiders is the theme of P.P. Mahto's essay. Through folk songs he has been able to highlight the tale of the suffering of the marginals whether it was their migration to Assam tea gardens or their displacement due to the opening up as well as the construction of dams. The author craves for the making of a New Jharkhand where every one will get job, every peasant will get irrigated lands, every student will be taught in their own mothertongue and the State will be free from corruption.

Sujata Singh explains that though the women of Jharkhand enjoyed considerable freedom in social life few women actually participated in the anti-colonial movement in Jharkhand. In Oraon folk song we find the names of Singi Dai and Kaili Dai who fought against the Turks at Rohtas during medieval period. Similarly during Santhal Hul, Birsa Movement and National Movement, we find the participation of tribal women. She points out that to ensure their participation in public life diffusion of education as well as political consciousness among the tribal women of Jharkhand is necessary.

C.K. Paty highlights the zamindari exploitation of the indigenous people in the nineteenth century Chotanagpur. During this period Christian Missionaries opened many schools which educated the tribals. The new education emboldened the indigenes against the tyranny. The result was that the tribal who lost their lands during the uprising of 1857-58 asserted their right over the Bhuinhari lands which the zamindars had usurped from them long before. Thus there started an affray against the zamindars leading to the origin of *Sardari Larai* which became the base of the gigantic movement by Birsa Munda.

A.K. Chattoraj in his chapter explains that during the second half of the nineteenth century there occurred a movement in Chotanagpur which is known as *Mulkui Larai* in which through petition to the British Government, Munda and Oraon Sardars tried to reoccupy their Bhuinhari lands from the zamindars which they had usurped from them long before. Though Christian Missionaries also helped them, tribals did not succeed in getting back their lost lands. They were duped by the lawyers of Calcutta. Their failure was attributed also to the lack of powerful leadership and strong organization. However, they were waiting for a leader and after some time Birsa entered the scene and he faught for the land. The difference between the above movement and that by Birsa Munda is that while the Sardari Larai was not anti-government the Birsa Movement was anti-government movement in nature.

Joseph Bara defines the tribal identity of the Munda and Oraons of Jharkhand during different periods. Sometimes they were termed as *dasyu* or *daitya* also and were treated as low class people. However, these indigenous people lived happily till the advent of Nagbansi rulers who subordinated them to the Raja and allowed their lands to be grabbed by the outsiders. In the mean time Christianity came here and under its influence tribals asserted their right over Bhuinhari lands and their separate identity.

P. Sen argues that in view of the contemporary concern among the *adivasis* of Jharkhand for their distinct religious community represented by *Sarna Dharam* the religious content of socio-religious movements has acquired a new meaning. Hence, instead of apprehending this content as a mere assertion of the autonomous political identity of the indigenes it should be studied as an important stage of their belief system. By a diachronic and synchronic analysis of the religious data of the movements she has been able to focus on the necessary links between the religious faith of the earlier and present movements. She has succeeded thereby in highlighting the underlying logical structure of the indigenous belief system as a basis of their identity claim.

The next essay by late Fr. Mathew Areeparampil makes a break in the narration of tribal movements to describe the backdrop that triggered the movements thematised by the last two chapters. He maintained that the tribals of Chotanagpur are the original settlers of this region who had always revolted against the dispossession of their lands by others. Since pre-colonial time, these indigenous people are very much attached to the nature. But due to the opening of different mines and dams they were not only dispossessed from their lands but also they had lost their identity, culture and their values. He raised the question how long these indigenous would continue to be victimized in the name of development.

Asha Mishra concentrates on the creation of a new State as the result of a continuous struggle of indigenous people of Jharkhand. During the whole twentieth century indigenous people of Jharkhand participated in various movements for the protection of their right over land, which strove for the creation of a separate State and ultimately they succeeded in their goal and a separate State of Jharkhand was created.

Lalita Sundi explains the importance of *jal, jungle* and *jameen* in the life of the *adivasi* of Jharkhand. She explores various forest rules which curtailed the right of indigenous people. For this they launched social protest during pre- as well as post-colonial periods. So, she argues, that the history of Jharkhand is the history of unrelented struggle of the *adivasis* for the protection of their right over *jal, jungle* and *jameen.*

*Chaibasa* **Asha Mishra**
*20th February, 2009* **Chittaranjan Kumar Paty**

# Acknowledgements

This anthology owes much to several persons and sources. First of all, we are thankful to all the contributors, whose research papers have been included in the present monograph. We are grateful to UGC, Eastern Regional Office, Kolkata for their financial assistance without which the conference and this publication would not have taken shape. I am obliged to Dr. S.N.M. Topno, the Principal of Mahila College, Chaibasa, for her active help in this regard. We have no words to thank Dr. Asoka Kumar Sen for his invaluable help in the making of this monograph. We extend our grateful thanks to Dr. Padmaja Sen, Dr. Shailbala Das, Mrs.T. Bibi, Dr. S. Prasad and Dr. D. Chakraborty for their help in organizing the conference. Thanks are also due to Dr. Shashilata, Mrs S. Dei, Dr. M.K. Jaiswal, Dr. C.R. Dey, and S.K. Dey who helped me from time to time. We feel pleasure in thanking all those who directly or indirectly helped us in achieving our goal. In this connection we would like to gratefully acknowledge the support provided by Sri Nand Lal Rungta, an eminent industrialist and philanthropist of this region. We are also thankful to Sri Ajai Prasad and his associates of C.M.C. Computer Education, Chaibasa for the preparation of monograph.We thank Sri Abhijit Gaurav Paty, Support Engineer, Chaibasa for his help during the conference. At the end we express our heartfelt thanks to all the members of our family for their active support towards completion of this project.

**Asha Mishra**
**Chittaranjan Kumar Paty**

# Contents

# List of the Contributors

**A.K. Chattoraj,** Reader, Department of History, Ranchi College, Ranchi.

**Asha Mishra,** Reader and Head, Department of History, Mahila College, Chaibasa.

**Asoka Kumar Sen,** Independent Researcher of Tribal History

**Chittaranjan Kumar Paty,** former Reader and Head, Department of History, Tata College, Chaibasa.

**Indra Kumar Choudhary,** Professor, Department of History, Ranchi University, Ranchi.

**Joseph Bara,** Fellow, Indian Institute of Advanced Studies, Shimla.

**Lalita Sundi,** Rajeev Gandhi National Fellow, Department of History, Ranchi University, Ranchi.

**Mathew Areeparampil,** Former Director, Tribal Research and Training Centre, Lupungutu, Chaibasa.

**Padmaja Sen,** Reader and Head, Department of Philosophy, Mahila College, Chaibasa.

**Pashupati Prasad Mahato,** Chairman, Anthropology Research Committee, Indian Academy of Social Sciences & Member, Anthropology Sub-committee, The Asiatic Society.

**Sujata Singh,** Lecturer, Department of History, Ranchi University, Ranchi.

# 1

# Resurrecting A Tribal Leader from Oblivion

## *Gono Pingua and the Revolt of 1857-59*

ASOKA KUMAR SEN*

Reconstructing the history of *adivasi*[1] movements in assertion of political identity has recently surfaced as a world-wide trend among scholars across disciplines. But it has generally been characterised by a hegemonising mindset when it is studied within the framework of nationalist movement, denying thereby the autonomy and space these deserve.[2] While doing so these often treat tribe as a faceless aggregate bereft of agency and organisation.[3] The other and more recent trend is to reconstruct the history of Indian indigenes to claim a rightful place in Indian history.[4] But the latter also provides an inadequate narrative mostly because of hegemonisation of a different type. Here anti-British tribal movements are historicised around some cult figures like Ganga Narain (Bhumij Revolt), Sido and Kanu (Santal *Hul*), Arjun Singh (rebellion of 1857-58 in Singhbhum) and Birsa Munda

---

* This paper owes both for facts and sometimes in expressions to author's unpublished papers 'Reconstructing an Event: The Great Rebellion of 1857-58 and the Singhbhum Indigenes' and 'Contesting Marginalization: Colonial Representation of the Indigenes in the Great Rebellion of 1857-58', presented at the *International Conference on Contesting Identities: Tribes, Indigenous Peoples and Adivasis in Colonial and Postcolonial India,* organised by Department of History, Visva Bharati, Santiniketan, 26-27 November, 2005.

(*Ulgulan*),[5] in close conformity to nationalist historiographic tradition where the like of Mahatma Gandhi, Jawaharlal Nehru *et al.*, are assigned prime positions while others are neglected. Consequently these studies fail to specify how these regional movements were organised with support from sub-regional levels and the leadership that mobilised the same.

This chapter while contesting[6] the hegemonising tendency of the latter variety seeks to focus on tribal leadership and organisation at the sub-regional level. The person chosen for this is Gono (Gonoo in the archival source) Pingua, the ethnic leader from Patajaint in Kolhan of erstwhile Singhbhum in the Revolt of 1857-59. We did not have any knowledge about him till recently[7] because of the elitist historiographical approach and the inadequate resources these works invoked. The essay first explores both oft trodden and untrodden materials to relate the extent and cause of the erasure of Gono in oft used sources and then extrapolates strategic materials to rescue the tribal leader from oblivion. Next it conducts the crucial act of configuring the man to understand the part played by him, the distinguishing character of ethnic leadership and the linkage between the regional and central leadership. So while studying the role of a tribal leader in the revolt the essay relates the generic phenomenon of ethnic leadership and the social milieu that sustained or clogged it.

## Examining the Sources

Broadly speaking we have in hand three types of sources. Though there is a commonality in their being colonial in origin, we find perceptible difference in recording due to the changed occasions and time of their origin. The first represented the letters and correspondences of British officials during and after the insurrection followed by the sketchy ethnographic narrations prepared on their basis.[8] We notice a complete erasure of the role of Gono Pingua in this source. This forces us to cull the judicial recordings in 1864[9] containing the depositions of witnesses and arguments recorded during Gono's trial.[10] Being a product of the proceedings of court room, this source, which I term the testimonial-memory, obviously lacked objectivity as the witnesses were either pro-government or forced by circumstance to be so, while Gono was keen to refute the charge of treason. But being a trial-document it recorded the voices of tribal participants, both anti- and pro-British, who provides, direct knowledge about the uprising and its ethnic leader. Thus it constitutes an important, and perhaps the only substantial source material on him. There is yet a third source which has so far remained untapped. This is the *Khuntkatti* papers[11] related to the Tuckey land revenue settlement (1913-18). Though this source specifically deals with Kolhan *raiyats'* right of *khuntkatti*[12] we come across sparse yet significant reminiscences of villagers about the uprising of 1857-58 and its leaders Arjun Singh and Gono. Significance lies not because it adds to the existing corpus but because it informs us about strategy of recalling an event, its centrality in rural life and the importance that the people accorded to the above leaders.[13] These three sources have been invoked in the present writing to reconstruct the crucial role of Gono in organising and intensifying anti-British struggle of 1857-58.

## Story of the Ethnic Leader Relegated to Oblivion

When we examine the first source we discern the play of a strategy of knowledge appropriation and construction which had a distinct imperialist and elite overtone. The event was considered as an anti-British rebellion and only politico-military account was produced with the focus on the key players, the British as well as the feudal elements. So British administrator-generals like Birch as well as Dalton and Arjun Singh, Raja of Porahat as leader of the rebellion, and his men occupied almost the entire stage. Even with the empiricism of the basic civil character of the event the chroniclers did not care to dilate on how this civil rebellion was ethnically mobilised and led.

Similarly, the memory of Gono is both sparse and frugal in the *Khuntkatti* papers. What is significant is that diminution of Gono in social memory was accompanied by the recession of the rebellion from social centre-stage. Out of a total of 904 villages in Kolhan only a few[14] remembered the event either independently or along with the disturbances of 1830-37.[15] Villagers merely recalled the 'disturbance in Raja Arjun Singh's time' and the exodus of the Bhuiyans from their villages with almost no further information. Gono's memory survived in his natal village[16] and that too not as the village tradition. We learn that Gono had participated in the uprising as an adherent of Arjun Singh; he ran away from the village and was later caught and transported. Putkar Pingua, Gono's son, related

> 'during the time of the mutiny the Hos fought with the Raja and the Sahibs came and burned our village and we all ran away. I was young then and the village remained empty for a year...My father Gono was caught with the Raja and was transported. Several men were caught and hanged and several were transported.'

The other informant was his co-villager Kasi Gour who while corroborating the above information added that Gono was caught with the Raja at Jeraikela.[17] Significantly the rebel leader was recalled as 'my father' (Putkar's testimony) and 'father of Putkar' (Kasi Gour's testimony).[18] Gono and his insurgency were remembered collaterally to determine whether Pingua *killi*, the founder or *Khuntkattidar* of Patajaint village, was in continued possession of the village. Determination of *Khuntkatti* right and not anti-British rebellion being the term of reference this source obviously suffers from lack of details about the uprising. But the recall was impacted equally by the constraint of the present. Since after the failure of the tribal uprising of 1857-58 the indigenes of Kolhan had finally surrendered to British rule and loyalty to the British was more real and existentially imperative. So present generation tended not to be emotive about the disloyalty shown during 1857-58. This enacted the 'politics of forgetting' resulting in the emasculation of the Great Revolt and Gono in popular memory. Invoking trial recordings in resurrecting and reinstating Gono Pingua in the forefront of regional history, therefore, becomes necessary.

## Cruciality of Judicial Papers in Resurrecting Gono

Gono's resurrection was facilitated thankfully to the subalternist historiographic focus on the tribe and Prof. Gautam Bhadra's short but seminal essay based primarily on the informed judicial papers. This source provides details which enabled us to configure Gono both socially and as an ethnic leader of the civil rebellion in Kolhan. But to fulfil this crucial task selective invocation of other sources is necessary both for substantiation and corroboration.

In his judgment of 9 March 1864, E.T. Dalton, Commissioner of Chotanagpur, considered Gono 'the most active adherent of the ex Raja of Porahat amongst Singhbhum or *Larka Kols* and the principal agent in spreading disaffection amongst them and the leader of the men of that tribe.'[19] The depositions of different witnesses reveal that the memory of the leader of indigenous insurgency was not only vivid[20] but also pervasive, extending beyond Patajaint, his natal village, to other such villages as Deoposi, Konslapose, Gamharia, Kochra and Uligutu in Kolhan and Baljuri in Bamanghatty *pargana* of Mayurbhanj. We learn that Mata was the father of Gono. Mata and his elder son had fought against the British in 1837. He was subsequently imprisoned and later he died in jail, while his son was awarded capital punishment.[21] Gono was a literate man having been taught at Chaibasa school. But due to poverty he had to discontinue his studies and take to 'evil' ways. We can presume that due to insurgency, Mata was deprived of the Mundaship and property that distressed the family. What motivated him to join insurgency was not related. But we can imagine that the family tradition of anti-British resistance and the punishment of his father and brother, along with the subsequent impoverishment of his family, provided the trigger.

## Gono as Raja's Associate and Leader of Ethnic Insurgency

Anti-British uprising[22] in Singhbhum began from Chaibasa, the headquarters of the district, when British sepoys stationed there mutinied, looted the treasury and set off for Ranchi to join with the mutineers there. Sissmore, the assistant political agent, posted at Chaibasa, left his station. This created a political void which inspired Arjun Singh's men to hoist the Raja as the lord of the land. They also began anti-British preparations by issuing instructions to the traders to provide ration, employed local blacksmiths to prepare cannon balls and circulated battle arrow in villages to mobilise popular, particularly ethnic, support. This brought Gono in the scene, first as the associate and then as the mobiliser and leader of ethnic upsurge. He accompanied some Mundas and Mankis to Porahat, met Arjun Singh and responded to his call to join the rebellion.[23]

Before detailing his role it is relevant to understand why Gono and his kin joined anti-British rebellion under Arjun Singh. It has been fashionable in elite historiography to characterise subaltern insurgency either as driven by momentary impulse or elite-inspired.[24] This approach denies, like others, the adivasis also of either consciousness or agency. It is true that the Raja commanded respect of the indigenes in Singhbhum. But as I have shown in an earlier essay that grievance against the exotic land revenue and judicial systems created social ferment which manifested in their hiding of the *hals* to avoid payment of land rents.[25] But their defeat and subsequent punitive measures that Wilkinson unleashed[26] so detracted the Ho of Kolhan-Porahat that they needed outside help to start anti-British rebellion. However, the other side of the picture was that the relationship between non-tribal Raja and the adivasis was mutually beneficial and sustaining. So, as related before, the Raja solicited indigenous help and a section of social leadership responded to it. This can be corroborated by Gono's testimony quoted below.

> 'The whole country was in revolt and Passes were held against the British, and there was fighting by order of the Rajah Urjoon Singh. All the Moondahs and Mankis went to the Rajah, I was with them; the Rajah asked us what we were going to do. We replied that the Sahibs have run away and you are now our ruler we will hold

> to you....Afterwards the Rajah called us and said, "see I have been hunted from Chuckerdhurpore and from Porahat and now obliged to live in the jungles. What will you do? Will you fight for me?" We said, "we would fight and swore to do so."[27]

The Raja appointed Gono as his 'Sirdar in Singhbhum' by investing him with the *'tal-pat'* (palm leaf) letter, a turban and a horse.[28] This was presumably caused by the knowledge of his family background and Gono's turbulent ways. But the question is why should Gono need the investiture? It leads us to characteristic lack in tribal leadership. Though Ho resistance had been socially organized these generally suffered from the absence of a centralized leadership. This forced them to fight the enemy at area levels under regional leaders. So we meet such leaders as Poto Sardar, Narra, Burrai, Borah and Pandua and not one representing the whole community during 1836-37.[29] On the other hand the emergence of supreme leaders like Sidu and Kanu in the *Hul* and Birsa in the *Ulgulan* was achieved only by invoking divine sanction. Poto Sardar followed the same strategy.[30] Gono assumed this position through the trans-ethnic secular command of the investiture as the 'Sirdar in Singhbhum' by Arjun Singh. This seemingly legitimized Gono's position as the acclaimed leader of ethnic revolt in south Kolhan. But he had to adopt different modalities to mobilise villagers.

During Kol rebellion (1830-32), Santal *Hul* (1855-56) and Birsite *Ulgulan* (1895-1900) ethnic mobilization was achieved through the circulation of the battle arrow, leaf cups containing *tel-sindur* (oil and vermillion powder) and beating of the drum.[31] Gono however followed none of them but either himself or instructed his agents to make use of the palm leaf letter to garner the support of villagers for him. Martum deposed *'Gono had in his hand a tal-pat letter, which he said was an order from the ex-Rajah and asked if in obedience to it we would assemble a force and take up a portion of Juggernathpore or not.'*[32] Interestingly that a literate symbol be invoked by Gono to sway an oral society in his favour amply spoke of the impact of writing,[33] reminiscent of Sidu and Kanu's application of the similar strategy during Santal *Hul.* The other strategy was to resort to strong-arm tactics of terrorizing people including village heads to join or suffer in case of recalcitrance. Chamroo, a Ho resident of Uligutu village, and Manki, informed :

> 'Gonoo asked for my father, but he had left the village. Then he ordered me to collect cattle to yoke in the Suggars. He threatened to burn the village. I gave both, and he took off all the boxes....A very large body of insurgents were with Gonoo... they filled the village and were in every house demanding food and drink... I had not seen Gonoo before, but they said this is Gonoo our leader, don't you know him, and what he will do to you if you disobey. He threatened me himself and abused my mother.'[34]

Consequently Gono's name 'was not only in every body's mouth' but his writ ran across the entire region, forcing the Mankis, Mundas and villagers to generally obey him. Gono became an itinerant man trotting between Porahat and Kolhan. He collected 100 armed Hos to assist Arjun Singh in Porahat. From there he returned to Jayantgarh where under his orders the murder of a *jamadar* (labour-contractor) and two *barkandazs* (guards) were committed. This was a singular event which acted as 'the signal for an outbreak in Southern Kolhan'. The British force under the special commissioner and other officials countered this by arresting two minor rebel leaders.[35] Gono then went back to the Raja and returned to Kolhan once again to mobilize support for him. Insurgents looted the provisions sent from Chaibasa by the British, which Gono arranged to send to the Raja loaded in bullock carts. This was followed by the historic fights at Mogra and Seringsia, led by Gono. At Mogra, Ho insurgents compelled the British to change their route of movement. While crossing a dry stream about 4,000 arrow-clad men launched a fierce attack on the British force in which Capt. Hale received critical injuries while Lt. Birch's arm was pinned to his side by an arrow. In all 150 Hos laid down their lives, while only one Sikh soldier was killed and about 26 were critically injured. Undaunted by heavy casualty, the insurgents chased the enemy for seven miles against the volley of gunshots fired by the retreating enemy. This forced the British to requisition the help of *shekhawati* battalion from Raniganj and an additional force of 100 European soldiers. But this mobilization failed to daunt the rebels of Kolhan and Porahat who continued their heroic fight. Under Gono's leadership the historic resistance was organized at Seringsia *ghat* (pass). Unfortunately testimonies fail to historicise the full details. Rather those by Gono and his adherent Rainso, obviously to escape punishment, tried to impress that rebels abandoned the pass at the sight of a large force under Birch without offering the fight.[36] On the other hand, by piecing together information provided by other witnesses we are able to show how comparatively resourceless but ingenious ethnic leader planned his strategy to outwit more formidable and resourceful adversary. He deliberately chose Seringsia pass for the strategic reason to offer resistance. He collected and headed 'a large body of insurgents', numbering about 200- 300 armed men, and encamped there for six days waiting for the British force. His adherents captured a person of European origin whom Gono ordered to be executed. To intimidate opponents he "made sham guns by placing plantain trees on 'Suggars' ".[37]

What is interesting to note is that though Gono considered himself the representative of the Raja and act on his behalf, he sported himself as the 'Chief of Singbhoom', riding the horse given to him by the Raja himself.[38] Though Raja's investiture strengthened and legitimised his position, the awe that his turbulent ways had evoked and the force of his personality definitely impacted Gono's ascent as the central commander of ethnic upsurge of south Kolhan displaying considerable freedom of action yet reinforcing anti-British insurgency under Arjun Singh. For waging war against the Queen and for causing the death of a European, Gono Pingua was sentenced to life imprisonment u/s 121 and 302 IPC.[39]

## Conclusion

What emerges from the surfing of diverse sources is that correspondences, reports and ethnographies of the Great Revolt of 1857-58 which have so far dominated historical reconstruction need to be supplemented by other sources used in this essay. It may help us in truly understanding the nuances of tribal movements, nay of popular movements in general. In the present case the elitist representation lionising the correspondences etc. gets contended when we explore and examine the judicial papers. What surfaces from here is the near complete picture of a sub-regional leader who was both part of the district level struggle under Arjun Singh yet independent of it, who strengthened the generic movement yet replenished Ho tradition of anti-British militancy. In fine the essay seeks to emphasise that to understand the basic social character of adivasi assertion for political identity it is time to look beyond the cults of Sidu, Kanu, Arjun Singh and Birsa and resurrect the regional-level figures like Gono Pingua and then to delve further to historicise the role of many other faceless adherents.[40] One may yet be inspired by the history of tribe-non-tribe collaboration (Arjun Singh and all his men and Patan Goala as Gono's adherent) to configure tribal movements in Jharkhand also as attempts to assert both ethnic and trans-ethnic identity of the social marginals and Jharkhandis in general.[41]

### NOTES

1. Tribe and adivasi have been used in this essay as synonyms.
2. R.C. Majumdar, *History of the Freedom Movement in India,* Vol. I. *Firma* KLM, Calcutta, 1962, pp. 196-99.
3. For a critique of this approach see my 'Contesting Marginalization'.
4. We can mention the trend-setting work by K.K. Datta of pre-independence origin. K.K. Datta, *The Santal Insurrection of 1855-57,* University of Calcutta Press, Calcutta, 1940. It was later followed by J.C. Jha, *Kol Insurrection in Chotanagpur, Calcutta,* 1964; (K). S. Singh, *The Dust-Storm and the Hanging Mist, Firma* K.L. Mukhopadhyay, Calcutta, 1966; D.N. Baskey, *Saontal*

*Ganasangramer Itihas*, Pearl Publishers, Calcutta, 1982, (1976).

5. K.K. Datta, *The Santal Insurrection of 1855-5;* D.N. Baskey, *Saontal Ganasangramer Itihas;* J.C. Jha, *The Bhumij Revolt, 1832-33,* Munshiram Manoharlal, Delhi, 1967; (K). S. Singh, *The Dust-Storm and the Hanging Mist.*
6. The idea is, however, not to challenge the historic significance of their role. On the other hand it appreciates attempts already made to resurrect and assign them their due place in the mainstream historiography of Indian nationalism. But the author also believes that the on-going tradition of regionalizing of history will be enriched if we study the organization and leadership at sub-regional levels.
7. G. Bhadra, 'Four Rebels of Eighteen-Fifty-Seven', *Subaltern Studies IV,* Oxford University Press, Delhi, 1990, pp. 256-63; A.K. Sen, 'Ek Aitihasik Charitrer Anusandhan' in G. Roy (ed.), *Singhbhum Sahitya,* Jharkhand Sankhya, Sharad Sankalan, Chakradharpur, 1409 (BS), October 2002, pp. 57-62; A.K. Sen, 'Contesting Marginalization'; S. Das Gupta, 'Rebellion in a Little Known District of the Empire', in Sabyasachi Bhattacharya (ed.), *Rethinking 1857,* Orient Longman, New Delhi, 2007.
8. Letter of Lt. R.C. Birch, the Senior Assistant Commissioner, Singhbhum District to the Secretary to the Government of Bengal, Fort William, 6 October 1857, No. 40, Spare Copies of Porahat Papers (SCPP); Letter from Officiating Commissioner of Manbhum and Singhbhum to the Secretary to the Government of Bengal, 29 December 1857, SCPP, from 1857 to 1862, No. 31, Bihar State Archives (BSA); Letter from E.T. Dalton, Commissioner of Chotanagpur to E.H. Lushington, Secretary to the Government of Bengal, 30 September 1859, SCPP, No. 224, BSA; W. Gray, Secretary to the Government of India, Home Department to W.S. Seton-Karr, Secretary to the Government of Bengal, 18 April 1861, SCPP, No. 759, BSA; E.T. Dalton, *Tribal History of Eastern India* (original title Descriptive Ethnology of Bengal), Cosmo Publication, Delhi, 1973, (1872), pp. 183-84; C.E. Buckland, *Bengal under the Lieutenant-Governors from 1854-1898,* Calcutta, 1902, pp. 98-109; F.B. Bradley-Birt, *Chota Nagpore A Little Known Province of the Empire,* London, 1903, pp. 219-28.
9. From Lieutenant-Colonel E.T. Dalton, Commissioner of Chota Nagpore to F.R. Cockerell, Officiating Secretary to the Governor of Bengal, No. 437, 15 March 1864, Judicial Department, Proceeding No. 31, Judicial Department, May 1864. West Bengal State Archives (WBSA).
10. Testimonies of Gonoo, Martum, Konka, Rainso, Bhagwan, Chamroo, Soma, Ramoo and Rajoo Chaprasi, *Ibid.*

11. Tuckey Settlement Village Papers included *Khuntkatti* Reports, Papers of cases under sections 83 and 85, Tanaza Papers and Village Notes. These have been preserved at the District Record Room, Chaibasa, West Singhbhum, Jharkhand in village related *vastas* or bags, excluding, however, the bound volumes of the Village Notes.
12. It is the right that devolved on the family founding a village from primeval forests.
13. These aspects have been elaborated in my unpublished paper 'Reconstructing an Event'.
14. Exact number of the villages cannot be provided both because of the vastness as well as the non-availability of the papers. It can only be presumed that the number was not very high.
15. For details see M. Sahu, *The Kolhan under the British Rule,* Calcutta, 1986, pp. 40-45, 71-83.
16. Tuckey Settlement *Khuntkatti* Papers (TSKP) of Patajaint, *Vasta* No. 45, Kolhan *thana,* pp. 3-7.
17. *Ibid.* According to another source Gono was arrested in Goodri. Gonoo's Testimony.
18. TSKP of Patajaint, pp. 3-7.
19. Remarks by the Commissioner of Chota Nagpore on the trial of Gonoo, son of Mata, Judicial Department, Proceeding No. 31.
20. We may attribute this vividness to temporal proximity. For time-span altering message-content see J. Vansina, *Oral Tradition As History,* London, James Curry, 1985, p. 54.
21. Testimonies of Martun and Rainso.
22. For details see Sahu, *The Kolhan,* pp. 84-95; S.K. Sen, *Tribal Struggle for Freedom: Singhbhum 1820-1858,* Concept Publishing Company, New Delhi, 2008, pp. 82-107.
23. Gonoo's Testimony.
24. A recent study for instance observes that Ho insurgency was 'instigated by the old royal family' and the Ho succumbed to it due to 'several linkages between the elite ruling class and their tribal subjects'. S. Das Gupta, 'Rebellion in a Little Known District of the Empire', pp. 110-11.
25. 'Reconstructing an Event.
26. In fact Wilkinson became the symbol both of 'mildness and firmness', as is evident in Lt. Birch invoking his predecessor in a meeting of Kolhan villages summoned by him to dissuade them from militancy. Letter of Lt. R.C. Birch, the Senior Assistant Commissioner, Singhbhum District to the Secretary to the Government of Bengal, Fort William, 6 October 1857, No. 40, para. 10.
27. Gonoo's Testimony.
28. Rainso's Testimony.

29. A contemporary source, while noting Poto of Rajabassa village and others as instigators, named him as well as Narra, Borah and Pondooa of Bulundia and Burrai of Kharband as the 'leaders' of ethnic resistance during 1836-37. *The Asiatic Journal and Monthly Register for the British and Foreign India, China and Australia,* Vol. XXVI, New Series, May-August, 1838, London, 1838. See also C.P. Singh, 'The Martyrs of Singhbhum', *The Journal of the Bihar Research Society,* Vol. LVII, January-December, 1971, Parts I-IV, pp. 149-53.
30. Poto employed a Bhuiyan priest named Mangani Naik who issued charmed arrows to be circulated in Ho country and distributed such charms as would render the wearer invulnerable and British guns innocuous. *Ibid.*
31. R. Guha, *Elementary Aspects of Peasant Insurgency in Colonial India,* Oxford University Press, Delhi, 1983, pp. 118-24, 233-35, 238.
32. Testimonies of Martun and Konka.
33. Ajay Skaria, 'Writing, Orality and Power in the Dangs, Western India, 1800s-1920s', *Subaltern Studies IX,* Oxford University Press, Delhi, 1997, pp. 13-55.
34. Testimony of Chamroo.
35. They were Jiba and Charee, who were convicted of the charge of murdering the police personnel and convicted. Testimony of Konka.
36. Testimonies of Gonoo and Rainso.
37. Remarks by Dalton; Testimonies of Konka and Bhugwan. For Kolhan uprising see Dalton to Lushington, paras. 33-4; Dalton, *Tribal History,* p. 184; Gray to Seton-Karr, para. 18; Buckland, *Bengal under the Lieutenant-Governors,* pp. 105-6; Sahu, The *Kolhan,* pp. 84-95.
38. Testimonies of Martun, Rainso, Chamroo, Konka and Remarks by the Commissioner of Chotanagpur.
39. Judgement of E.T. Dalton.
40. They may be Patan Goala, an active adherent of Gono, whose name figured both in the dispatch and the deposition as well as Gooda Manjee, Jiba and Charee. Gray to Seton-Karr, para. 16; Deposition of Konka.
41. Guha, *Elementary Aspects,* pp. 22-23; R.D. Munda & S. Bosu Mullick (eds.), *The Jharkhand Movement : Indigenous Peoples' Struggle for Autonomy in India,* IWGIA and Birsa, Document No. 108, Copenhagen, 2003, Introduction, pp. vii-ix.

2

# Situating the Tribes of Palamau in the Revolt of 1857-58 in Jharkhand

INDRA KUMAR CHOUDHARY

Situating tribes in the uprising of 1857 in Jharkhand has emerged in recent decades as an important trend in historical research.[1] It has significantly revealed regional variations retaining however some broad commonalities. While the emergence of feudal and *jagirdari* systems and the subjection to British rule bound the regions together, differences might be witnessed in the extent and nature of feudal system, rivalries among local chiefs, the hold of the tribal communities on the body politic, inter-relation between the tribal communities and the local chiefs, depth of missionary penetration and the differential linkage with the mainstream movement. Consequently when we seek to reconstruct the history of the Revolt of 1857-58 we cannot ignore the regional diversities. So what we find in the region of Ranchi may not be seen at Hazaribagh, Santal Pargana, Palamau and Singhbhum. Of these important centres of the Revolt in Jharkhand this chapter has taken up Palamau to relate the civil uprising staged by two *adivasi* communities, the Bhogtas and Cheros under the leadership of two Bhogta leaders Nilambar and Pitambar. Though predominantly territorial in nature, it had uniquely a transcendent character for the attempt to forge a link with the mainstream uprising led by Kunwar Singh and his brother Amar Singh. Divided in three sections the first draws the historical setting, the second narrates the course of the uprising highlighting its broad territorial and transcendental specificities, while the third sums up the above noted details.

**The Milieu**

Before recounting the course of the uprising it is necessary to relate the broad issues that set the stage for the stormy movement. Most prominent was the urge among the Cheros and Bhogtas to revive the lost political supremacy which they had achieved in the past. The circumstances leading to the establishment of British rule in Palamau sowed the seeds of dissatisfaction and enmity between the dispossessed Cheros and the British. The Cheros and Kharwars of Palamau became feudal chiefs in the process of state formation. Population of Palamau then consisted of Kharwars, Gonds, Mars, Korwas Pahariyas and Kisans. Amongst them Kharwars were demographically most predominant. The Cheros conciliated them and allowed them to remain in peaceful possession of the hill tracts bordering Sarguja.[2] Bhagwant Rai was the first of a long line of Chero chiefs who reigned in Palamau for nearly 200 years. The first intervention of the British in the affairs of the Chero Raj of Palamau occurred in 1772 owing to protracted internecine quarrels (1722-70) between two rival Chero factions. The incapacity of the last Raja, Churamani Rai, the refractory conduct of the disaffected *jagirdars* and the mounting revenue arrears led to the estate being put up to auction and the Government purchased it for Rs. 51,000 in 1814. Finally, in 1814, on the recommendation of Major Roughsedge, then commanding the Ramgarh battalion, it was granted to Raja Ghanshyam Singh of Deo (in Gaya district) on an annual revenue of Rs. 9,000 as a reward of past services in quelling the Chero and Kharwar insurrections.[3] Thus the imposition of British rule gradually but inexorably led to the extinction of Chero kingship. The Cheros, however, were keen to regain their authority and when the great rebellion of 1831-32 broke out the Cheros and Kharwars took part in the uprising actively. Though the rising was soon quelled, they again got the opportunity in 1857. In this sense the participation of Cheros and the Kharwar in the revolt of 1857 seems to be motivated by an attempt to restore their former glory.

Political situation of Palamau was complicated by the crises of agrarian landlordism and feudal system. These fomented discontent of the *jagirdar* which led to their risings in 1800, 1817 and 1832. These were but the faint presages of the coming storm a few years later.[4] K.S. Singh observes "these successive uprisings directed not only against the established authority but also against the non-tribals and those who had conspired against the destroyed Chero kingdom, reflected an agrarian and political reality".[5] The *jagirdars* rose against the Company rule partly because the steep increase in revenue demand and partly because the property of *jagirdars* and under tenure-holders had been sold for arrears.[6] O'Malley also hinted at their decaying situation. He informed, "Cheros having thus established themselves, strengthened their position by conferring *jagirs* on their followers, and numbers of these *jagirdars,* with impoverished and deeply mortgaged estates still exist".[7] In fact the system of granting service *jagirs* had several negative effects. It has been reported that a large number of *jagirs* were given to Cherawans, Kharwar and Bhogats for military service. Other kind of *jagirs* too were given. The *jagirdars* who were called upon to render services paid exceedingly small revenue. This led to economic burden on general peasantry. Thus decaying economic condition of the Cheros added fuel to the fire. A large number of small Chero *jagirdars* in the district had come into existence and they had mostly mortgaged their small estates. Dalton held that many proprietors might have joined the insurgents to avoid their incumbrances.[8] Unlike Cheros, the Kharwars were largely peasants, and there were very few *jagirdars* among them. They have been called 'free-booters'[9] and 'lawless raiders'. These are the colonial words having an imperialistic overtone. In fact Bhogtas were freedom-loving people, restless to obtain their lost status. They were not satisfied by the small *jagirs* given to them. They, therefore, established a league with Chero *jagirdars* and decided to oust the British from Palamau. J.N. Sarkar observes "Just as the crusades were joined by many a debtor to escape from the clutches of money lenders of medieval Europe, so the Palamau *jagirdars* might have been tempted to join the movement with a similar object. This throws a new light on the genesis of the movement and would show that it had a 'sordid aspect' as distinct from the lofty national impulse of freeing the country from a foreign rule."[10]

Next was the traditional rivalry between Chero and Rajput chiefs which reached the height during pre-revolt decades. The traditional Chero-Rajput animosity was fanned by the Chero spirit of restoration. This unnerved local Rajput chiefs who decided to join the British to thwart the political designs of the Cheros. This led to an entente between the British government and Rajput thakurais.[11]

There were some administrative problems too. The people of Palamau suffered due to the prevailing administrative system. In 1842 the district headquarters were removed to Ranchi (Kishanpur) and the courts, already sufficiently remote, thus became still more inaccessible. In 1852 one of the Agent's[12] junior assistants was stationed at Koranda, on the Jamura Pat, within the Sarguja border from whence he exercised jurisdiction over pargana Palamau as well as Sarguja and Udaipur.[13] But Koranda was very remote from Palamau. In his letter No. 92 of 20 April 1859 Colonel Dalton reported to Government, "as statistics collected showed that it was by no means a healthy locality either for Europeans or for natives. The Palamau people complained not only of the long journey that they had to make, which could only be undertaken during the favourable seasons of the year, but the poverty of Koranda and its neighbourhood was such that they had to take with them provisions to last them during the whole period of their sojourn, and though Koranda, or Jamura Pat, was within the limits of Sarguja, it was for its inaccessibility, not more patronized by the Sarguja people than by the Palamau people."[14] While the people suffered due to the above process, the British were also put to discomfort. As the Junior Assistant of Governor-General's Agent, South-West Frontier, was stationed at distant Koranda, when in August 1857 the Ramgarh Battalion mutinied, there was no representative of the administration other than *tahsildar* nearer to Palamau to manage and lead the affairs.

Geo-polity of Palamau had a strong bearing on the course of the events. Palamau famous as 'the ancient gateway of Chotanagpur' was bounded on the north by the river Son which separated it from the districts of Sahabad and Gaya, on the east by the districts of Gaya and Hazaribagh, on the south by Gumla and Sadar subdivisions of Ranchi district, and on the west by the tributary state of Sarguja and the district of Mirzapur.[15] Due to its strategic location the ruling authorities were extremely keen that Palamau should be steered clear of all troubles and their rule solidly entrenched.[16] Tribal insurgency similarly was helped by the geo-political position of the area. Rebels chose the jungles and hills as their hideouts from where they launched attacks on the enemies and when the situation became adverse retreated into their booths for self-defence.

Tribal revolt of Palamau thrived and fostered under the able leadership of two brothers, Nilambar and Pitambar, the Bhogta *jagirdars* of Chemu and Saneya. Bhogtas were class of lawless raiders inhabiting the high plateau that lie on the borders of Sarguja. Cut off from the lowlands of Palamau by a range of hills of which they held in passes, they occupied an almost unassailable position.[17] The late chief of Bhogtas died an outlaw. On his death it was considered a wise policy to confer his territory in *jagir* on his sons Nilambar and Pitambar with nominal quit-rent. This policy was quite successful for the time being in suppressing the natural marauding tendencies of these chiefs.[18] But the pent up grievances of peasantry and local *jagirdars* were taken advantage of by these two brothers to mobilize and lead anti-British uprising of the *adivasis* and others during 1857-58.

While the stage was thus set, the trigger was set by the rising in Ranchi and Hazaribagh. Almost all contemporary sources confirm that Pitambar was at Ranchi when the outbreak took place. He, like many others, thought that British rule had come to an end.[19] This was confirmed by the behaviour of the two companies of the 8th Native Infantry who were then passing through Palamau to join Amar Singh. On his return to Palamau Pitambar and Nilambar gave the signal to the Bhogtas and Cheros to declare independence against British rule.[20] The turbulent but disgruntled tribes of Palamau did not fail to join their leadership. But of these tribes, deprived of their ancient line of chiefs, the Cheros were no longer 'the prime movers'. In fact the leading spirits were the Kharwars, and more especially a section of them known as the Bhogtas. Many of the Chero *jagirdars* agreed to join anti-British insurgency, partly on the promise of placing a Chero chief on the throne, partly, no doubt, in the hope of retrieving their old status and fortunes.[21] An important development was the conclusion of the Chero-Bhogta alliance. The last Chero-Raja, Churaman Rai, died childless, leaving a widow. On 26 September 1857 Babu Bhavani Baksh Rai came to Shahpur (opposite Daltonganj on the other side of the river Koel), residence of the widowed Rani. A general meeting of all the Chero chiefs was convened there. Whatever be the purpose of the meeting it was followed by a general rising both of Cheros and of Kharwars.[22]

**The Course of Events**

On 21 October 1857 a force of about 500 insurgents led by Nilambar and Pitambar made an attack on Chainpur, Shahpur and Lesliganj. The assault on Chainpur was directed against Raghubar Dayal and Kishan Dayal Singh to avenge an old animosity and also for their pro-British stance. But this was repulsed immediately.[23] Undaunted by this reverse, armed Cheros and Kharwars plundered the towns of Shahpur and Chainpur. The position of the *daroga* of Lesliganj and the *tahisildar* of Palamau became so precarious that they needed the protection provided by Thakur Kapilnath Singh. Thakur Raghubar Dayal, apprehending rebel attack, began preparations to ward it off. The activities of insurgent rebels reached alarming proportions,[24] the news of which was carried by two *chaprasis* (peons) of intelligence department. At this stage rebels were joined by about 300 mutineers of Sahabad.[25] They then marched to Shahpur, where they took possession of four guns belonging to Rani (wife of Raja Churaman Rai) and overpowered the police force in the local *thana*.[26] The next day they attacked Lesliganj (situated 10 miles east of Daltonganj). The British police and the artillery men fled away on their arrival and took shelter with Shivacharan Rai, a *jagirdar* of Nowagarh. At Lesliganj the rebels destroyed public buildings, pillaged the place and committed some murders.[27] Lieutenant Graham was directed to proceed quickly towards Lesliganj. The party to accompany Graham comprised some native officers, 8 hawaldars, 5 nayaks, 47 sepoys and five troopers. Though Dalton, the Commissioner of Chotanagpur, considered it a small force, he was confident that with the able assistance of loyal *zamindars* and *raiyats* of Palamau, Graham would be able to stem the crisis.[28] We however learn that further replenishment was considered necessary in the form of more than 50 men of the of Bengal police battalion[29] and 200 Europeans so that insurrection could be suppressed promptly.[30]

The panic in the British ranks is evident from British ethnography. Bradley Birt observed that but for two neighbouring loyal chiefs, Raghubar Dayal Singh and Kishan Dayal Singh, who held the fort of Chainpur, the Bhogtas would have swept the whole countryside unchecked.[31] By the end of November 1857, the whole country appeared to be up in the arms. Bhogtas created havoc in the region. With his small party Graham was shut up and besieged in the house of Raghubar Dayal Singh. The rebels set about plundering in all directions. Situation became so grave that on the request of Buckland, the then Lieutenant Governor of Bengal, two companies of 13th Light Infantry, which were at this time quartered at Sasaram, were directed to proceed under the command of Major Cotter to help Graham. Buckland at the same time also requested the Raja of Deo to furnish contingent for service in Palamau.[32] But the delay in the arrival of these forces put the rebels in an advantage.

The British authority was however determined to punish Nilambar and Pitambar around whom this insurgency had been organised. Rewards of rupees 300 each were offered for their apprehension. Meanwhile the insurgents had retreated into the jungles and hills of Palamau bordering on Sarguja. Dalton advised Graham not to enter the fastness of Bhogtas with the present small force. He also directed Lal Bindeswari Prasad Singh, the *subedar* of Sarguja, to keep 200 men in readiness on the border of Palamau so that Graham could obtain their services.[33] The situation was tense. Dalton was in touch with his intelligence network which gave him day to day information of Palamau. He authorized Graham to employ matchlock men. However, these measures could not change the situation up to 13 November 1857.[34] Nilambar and Pitambar again emerged from the hills and jungle and threatened second attack on Chainpur. But Graham escaped damage mainly due to the support of Raghubar Dayal Singh and Kishan Dayal Singh of Ranka. At this point Dalton visualised that the revolt of Nilambar and Pitambar could be suppressed only after getting services of Sikh soldiers at Hazaribagh or Madras detachment.[35] Meanwhile British force supported by the loyal zamindars, including that of Sarguja, unitedly faced Nilambar and Pitambar. However the united opposition of the enemies failed to dampen the spirit of these two leaders. On 18 November 1858, the rebels compelled the police force stationed at Burgar thana to retreat across the river Kanhar into Sarguja. The thana building was demolished by a section of the Bhogtas led by Bhoja and Bharat. The guard escaping to Sarguja across the Kanhar procured two adivasis as guides to conduct them by a narrow path through a long dense jungle right to the booths of insurgents. This surprise attack caused heavy casualty in which 16 rebels were killed, 30 wounded and 3 were made prisoners. Only three of the government forces were wounded.[36]

Undaunted by this reverse about 5,000 rebels launched an attack on the station of Rajhara on 27 November. Not only this they also targeted Messrs. Grundy and Malzar, the employees of the Bengal Coal Company, who had to make good their escape.[37] What is noteworthy of the rebel mobilization was that it comprised a large number of Brahmans, loyal to Chero leader Bhawani Baksh Rai. The rebels were however repulsed, many of them including about 500

Brahmans were apprehended and later subjected to various terms of imprisonment as well as hanging.[38]

On 30 November, much awaited two companies under Major Cotter crossed the river Son near Akbarpur and reached Shahpur on 8 December to help Graham. On the advance of the force the rebels retreated, but while retreating they burnt the village Manika, near Palamau fort. They also destroyed the house of Bhikhari Singh, a zamindar who had assisted Graham. A Coal Factory was also attacked by the insurgents. Graham, however, succeeded in apprehending several Bhogtas. To create fear among the people and deter them from further acts of insurgency an important Bhogta leader, who was a relative of the head-man, as well as Luckan Babu (Babu Debi Bux Rai, whom the insurgents wanted to make Raja of Palamau) and some other important leaders were hanged in front of the remains of the Lesliganj Thana.[39] This setback forced the rebels to withdraw from Chainpur. But they soon launched an attack on Ranka fort which was repulsed by Kishan Dayal. By this time Graham had received further reinforcement of 600 men, supplied by the Sarbarahkar of Sarguja. Moreover about 100 followers of Kishan Dayal, 300 men of Deo and 25 forces of Ramgarh battalion assisted him. Graham succeeded in capturing Premanand, *ilakadar* of Kunda and an influential leader of the Kharwar tribe, along with his followers.[40] The Bhogtas, who had meanwhile assembled near Magpurma ghat and fortified two other passes, plundered two villages under the leadership of Nilambar. He also waged guerrilla warfare from his jungle hideouts. He did not allow his enemies any opportunity of attacking him.[41] On the other hand, instead of making a frontal attack the British strategy was to cripple their resources and take possession of the estates and property of Bhogta leaders.[42]

Though the British authority had vested full powers to Graham to combat the situation Dalton himself proceeded to Palamau on 16 January 1858 and reached Manika on 21 January. They launched an attack on Palamau fort and compelled the rebels to flee, leaving guns, ammunition, cattle supplies and baggage behind them. While ten rebels laid down their lives, one British force was killed and two were wounded. Letters written by Amar Singh to Nilambar Sahi, Pitambar Sahi and Naklout Manjhi, a Kharwar and an arch enemy of the British, were found with baggage. These letters revealed that Amar Singh had promised insurgents immediate assistance from Kunwar Singh. These also testified that rebels of Palamau sought to coordinate with the rebels of Sahabad. The fact was that on several occasions the rebels of Sahabad entered Palamau and gave stiff challenge to the British authority. Not only this the strategy of rebels under Nilambar and Pitambar was to forge a link both with regional and provincial struggle. This was why a party of rebels from Palamau moved to Singhbhum to affect a junction with Porahat insurgents.[43] They were in league with Biswanath Sahi and Ganpat Roy of Ranchi who were exciting rebels in the bordering areas of Palamau near Nawagarh.[44]

Dalton remained at Lesliganj till 8 February 1858, collecting fresh supplies and making preparations with the aim of forcing the passes into the Bhogta country.[45] Meanwhile, he also issued *parwanas* for the attendance of loyal *jagirdars*. Though most of them reported to his call, Bhawani Baksh Rai of Bishanpur defied the order. As he was busy collecting a contingent to help the insurgents and his family committed various acts of treason, a reward of rupees 500 was announced for his apprehension so that he could be removed to Ranchi. Bhawani Baksh Rai also decided to surrender on 3 February 1858 as barring a few Bhogtas all the rebels had either been suppressed or punished. He begged mercy and agreed to send revenue to the authority. This way 'a principal obstacle' was removed.[46]

Dalton next decided to deliver the final blow on the Bhogta rebels. Having divided his force, he sent one body with Krishn Dayal Singh and others to Shahpur to advance towards Baghmara Ghat.[47] The other group under Graham came to know that the insurgents were plundering the village of Harnam in his immediate neighbourhood. He succeeded in intercepting the enemy, and rescuing a band of captives and a herd of cattle which they were in the act of driving off. Three prisoners were also taken, one a leader of some consequence. Two were hanged while the third was kept for the sake of information.[48] The British force reached Chemu (on the banks of the river Koel) on 13 February 1858. Chemu was the principal residence of Nilambar and Pitambar. The insurgent brothers had a fortified house there. Captain Dalton's force destroyed the village Chemu. The rebels deserted Saneya, another stronghold of close to Chemu. Large quantities of grain as well as cattle were seized. Several herdsmen, who had been captured by the rebels, were released. Though Dalton camped in Bhogta country till 23 February, he did not succeed in capturing Nilambar and Pitambar. Search parties were sent out in all directions and out of retaliation rebel villages were destroyed, goods and cattle were seized and their estates confiscated to the state.[49]

However, Nilambar and Pitambar were still beyond their reach. The nature of the terrain came to their temporary rescue. Bradley Birt writes, 'The great difficulty here, as elsewhere in Chotanagpur, was the nature of the country which offered such impenetrable retreats for the armed gangs into which the insurgents broke up after each defeat postponing their final subjugation to law and order until the latest possible movement'.[50] Though they continued their depredations for a time, they were both eventually captured and after full trial found guilty and hanged.[51] Their estates were confiscated under the Act XXV of 1857.[52] The British considered this a great achievement. Bradley Birt observed: 'The official note on the mutiny in Palamau closed with well-deserved tribute to the young British subaltern who had so worthily uphold the traditions of his race'.[53] However, the old English correspondence volume for 1860 shows that local opposition continued till 1860. Bhaiya Bhagwan Deo of Nagar Oantari refused to render military service to Government although bound to do so under the *sanad* on which he held his tenure. He was further charged for having supplied provision to the rebels who encamped near Nuggur (Nagar).[54] Thus the uprising in Palamau started in late 1857 but till 1860 which appears to be the longest period not only in the history of Jharkhand but also in Indian history.

## Conclusion

Thus the above narrative clearly indicates that the uprising in Palamau was diverse in nature. It was basically an ethnic upsurge of the Cheros and Bhogtas to fight the economic degradation caused by the land revenue and *jagirdari* system. It was no less an attempt to recover their ancestral domains and previous political status. The movement percolated to the masses, both ethnic and non-ethnic, which some of the *zamindars* and the principal men in the villages led. Participation of Ruttan Shah, Narayan Baniya, Kumkum Shah, Bhooka Shah, Ganpat, Manjhi, Kurtoo Manjhi as well as several Brahmans supported its demographically transcendent character.[55] Similarly while local issues provided the primary stimuli to underline its basic territorial character, as the uprising developed it assumed a spatially transcendent proportion as well for its linkage with rebels of Ranchi, Sahabad, Mirzapur, Hazaribagh and Singhbhum. This civil rebellion excelled also because of its leadership provided by Nilambar and Pitambar. The uprising of Palamau thus offers a unique example of subaltern and feudal[56] elements asserting their political identity against mighty British rule.

## NOTES

1. To note some of these works: K.K. Datta (ed.), *Unrest against British Rule in Bihar 1831-1859*, Patna, 1957; P.C. Roy Choudhury, 1857 *in Bihar (Chotanagpur and Santhal Parganas)*, Revenue Department Bihar, Patna, 1959; J.C. Jha, *Kol Insurrection in Chotanagpur*, Calcutta, 1964; (K). S. Singh, *The Dust-Storm and the Hanging Mist*, Firma K.L. Mukhopadhyay, Calcutta, 1966; P. Kumar, *Mutinies and Rebellions in Chotanagpur 1831-57*, Janaki Prakashan, Patna, 1991; S.K. Sen, *Tribal Struggle for Freedom: Singhbhum 1820-58*, Concept Publishing Company, New Delhi, 2008; N. Sur, 'Chotanagpur and the Rising of 1857', *Bengal Past and Present*, January-December, 1986,

pp. 28-62; G. Bhadra, 'Four Rebels of Eighteen-Fifty-Seven', *Subaltern Studies IV*, Oxford University Press, Delhi, 1990, pp. 256-63; S. Das Gupta, 'Rebellion in a Little Known District of the Empire', in Sabyasachi Bhattacharya (ed.) *Rethinking 1857*, Orient Longman, New Delhi, 2007, pp. 96-119.

2. L.S.S. O'Malley, *Bihar and Orissa District Gazetteers, Palamau*, Patna, 1926, p. 21.
3. P.C. Roy Chaudhury, *1857 in Bihar*, pp. 92-95.
4. P.C. Roy Chaudhury, *Bihar District Gazetteers*, Palamau, Secretariat Press, Patna, 1961, p. 70.
5. K.S. Singh, *Tribal Society in India*, Manohar, 1985, p. 32.
6. *Ibid.*
7. L.S.S. O'Malley, Bihar and Orissa District Gazetteers, p. 35.
8. Roy Chaudhury, *Bihar District Gazetteers, Palamau*, p. 76.
9. Buckland, *Bengal Under the Lieutenant Governors*, p. 118; F.B. Bradley-Birt, *Chotanagpur: A Little Known Province of the Empire*, Waterloo Place, London, 1910, p. 223.
10. Jagdish Narayan Sarkar, 'The Mutiny of 1857-58 and the Palamau Jagirdars', *The Journal of the Bihar Research Society*, Vol. XLI, December 1955, Part 4, p. 538.
11. K.S. Singh, *Tribal Society in India*, p. 32.
12. In 1854 the Agent was subordinated to the local government and renamed as Commissioner.
13. Roy Chaudhury, *1857 in Bihar*, p. 92.
14. T.W. Bridge, 'Final Report of the Survey and Settlement Operations in the District of Palamau 1913-1920', in Pandey R.N. Roy and Rajpal, *Manual of Chotanagpur Tenancy Laws* (arranged), Rajpal and Company Allahabad, 2001 (Reprint), p. 870.
15. Bridge, *Final Report*, p. 823.
16. Roy Chaudhury, *1857 in Bihar*, p. 103.
17. *Ibid.* p. 223; Buckland, *Bengal Under the Lieutenant Governors*, p. 118.
18. *Ibid.*
19. Bradley-Birt, *Chota Nagpur*, p. 223.
20. Buckland, *Bengal Under the Lieutenant Governors*, p. 118; E.T. Dalton to A.R. Young, Secretary to the Government of Bengal, No. 77 (Judicial) Dated Chota Nagpore, the 7th May 1858. Dalton reports, "Exaggerated accounts of Kunwar Singh's force and success have reached Palamau and caused an uneasy feeling there".
21. Buckland, *Bengal Under the Lieutenant Governors*, p. 118.
22. K.S. Singh, 'The Tribals and the 1857 Uprising', *Social Scientist*, Vol. 26, Nos. 104, Jnuary-April 1998. p. 78.
23. Buckland, *Bengal Under the Lieutenant Governors*, p. 118.
24. E.T. Dalton to A.R. Young, Secretary to the Government of Bengal, No. 64, (Judicial), Dated Chota Nagpore, 27 October 1857, and also No. 66, (Judicial), Dated Chota Nagpore, 28 October, 1857.

25. Ritambhari Devi, *Indian Mutiny : 1857 in Bihar*, Orient Publications, Delhi, 1989, p. 76.
26. K.K. Datta, *History of the Freedom Movement in Bihar*, Vol. I, Patna, 1957, p. 65.
27. Buckland, *Bengal Under the Lieutenant Governors*, p. 118.
28. Dalton to Young, No. 64 (Judicial), Dated Chotanagpore the 27th October, 1857, paras. 3-4.
29. Dalton to Young, No. 73. (Judicial), Dated Chota Nagpore, the 31st October, 1857.
30. *Ibid*, para. 3
31. Bradley Birt, *Chotanagpur*, p. 224.
32. *Ibid*. p. 225.
33. Dalton to Young, Secretary to the Government of Bengal No. 90, (Judicial), dated Chota Nagpore, the 12th November 1857.
34. *Ibid.*, No. 92 (Judicial), Dated 16th November 1857.
35. Dalton reports, "The Bhogtas had emerged from the hill and jungle collecting in large number under Pitambar and Nilambar and threatened a second attack on Chainpur.... Leiutenant Graham has the support of Thakurais.... Kishen Dayal Singh of Ranka, Raghubar Dayal Singh of Chainpur and Bhikaree Singh of Munika and others and I hope he will be joined by the Sarguja Manager and his force, of the Palamau Zamindars Babu Bhowany Bux Rai of Bisrampore and Bhagwan Singh of Gurwah are reported as not in attendance." E.T. Dalton to A.R. Young, No. 101, (Judicial) Dated Chota Nagpore; the 24th November
36. Roy Chaudhury, *Bihar District Gazetteers*, Palamau, p. 77.
37. Dalton reports, "Failing at Rajhara the Bhogta insurgents returned to their encamping ground in Lieutenant Graham's vicinity but on the 29th the main body moved off apparently in the direction of their homes. On the 30th they were halted on the Ormanjhi Nudi six miles from Lieutenant Graham's position at Chainpur and Cheroes and Khauwars were deserting them in large number". Dalton to A.R. Young No. 110 (Judicial) Dated Chota Nagpore the 4th December, 1857. Also Buckland, *Bengal Under the Lieutenant Governors*, p. 119.
38. Military (Proper) Proceedings, No. 415, Letter of Military Secretary of the Government of India, Dated 26 November, 1857, cited in B. Virottam, *Jharkhand Itihas Evam Sanskri*, Bihar Hindi Granth Ekadmi, Patna, 2001, p. 296.
39. Dalton to A.R. Young, No. 134 (Judicial) Dated Chota Nagpore, the 22nd December, 1857.
40. Dalton to A.R. Young, No. 121 (Judicial) Dated Chota Nagpore, the 11th December, 1857; Buckland, Bengal Under the Lieutenant Governors, p. 119; Colonel Malleson, Indian Mutiny, Vol. IV, W.H. Allen & Co., Waterloo Place, London, 1889, p. 305.

41. Buckland, *Bengal Under the Lieutenant Governors,* pp. 119-120.
42. Dalton informs, "The Lal Bindswary Prasad Singh Deo of Sarguja with his force was at Shahpore on the 25th December 1857 and was to have joined Lieutenant Graham at Lesliganj the next day. Thus reinforced Lieutenant Graham will have not less than 1600 armed men at his disposal." E.T. Dalton to A.R. Young, No. 141 (Judicial) Dated Chota Nagpore, the 29th December 1857.
43. Roy Chaudhury, *1857 in Bihar,* pp. 110-111
44. E.T. Dalton to A.R. Young, No. 128, (Judicial), dated Chota Nagpore, the 17th December, 1857. Dalton reports "For the last three days I have received report confirmatory of each other that the proclaimed rebels Gunpat Roy and Bishnath Thakur are lurking in the hills and jungles bordering on Palamau and that they are intriguing with the insurgent party in that parganna*s* and inciting them to make forays on rich places in Chota Nagpore hoping thereby to raise an insurrectionary feeling in this district."
45. Buckland, *Bengal Under the Lieutenant Governors,* p. 120.
46. *Ibid.,* p. 120.
47. Roy Chaudhury, *1857 in Bihar,* p. 99.
48. Buckland, *Bengal Under the Lieutenant Governors,* p. 121.
49. *Ibid.,* p. 121.
50. Bradlcy Birt, *Chotanagporc,* p. 226.
51. *Ibid.,* p. 226; O'Malley, *Bihar and Orissa District Gazetteers,* p. 40.
52. Datta, *History of the Freedom Movement in Bihar,* pp. 68-69.
53. Bradley Birt, *Chotanagpore,* p. 227.
54. Roy Chaudhury, *Bihar District Gazetteers, Palamau,* p. 86.
55. Roy Chaudhury, *1857 in Bihar,* pp. 112-113.
56. This happened in spite of the loyalty showed by feudal elements which adversely affected the solidarity of the civil population. We can list Raghubar Dayal Singh, Kishan Dayal Singh, Sheo Charan of Nawagarh, Bhikhari Singh of Manika, Bhagwan Deo of Untari and Bhaya Deo Nath Singh of Ontary who got reward and *khillat* for their loyalty.

# 3

# Assertion and Reassertion as Jharkhandi

## *A History of the Indigenous People 1763–2007*

PASHUPATI PRASAD MAHATO

Jharkhandi identity assertion has recently earned considerable academic as well as activistic response. Dr. Ram Dayal Munda (1993) observed :

> 'the struggles of the Indigenous and Tribal peoples centre around the issues of land, forests, water resources, culture and identity, directed towards their self-determination and finding a rightful place in the social, cultural, economic and political spheres of life in India.'

Similarly S. Bosu Mullick (1993) commented :

> 'The earliest known people were the Aryans who invaded the country of the indigenous peoples of India and subjugated them gradually through the ages.'

Mahato (1982, 1987, 2000) also remarked that the name used by the indigenous peoples for themselves was nothing else but the word meaning 'man'. But unfortunately the dominant societies have given the present names to most of the tribes in India having derogatory connotation.

In this backdrop it is pertinent to elaborate further the story of cultural marginalization of the indigenes as literarily depicted and to seek to know whether the marginalized could resist and combat the humiliation hurled on them by politically and culturally more dominant. Two sections of this chapter take up one by one the literary manifestations of cultural subjugation and the resistance the indigenes were able to offer.

## The Portrayal of the Indigenes

In the formative periods of the Aryan civilization the Aryan rulers generally called the subjugated peoples as the *dasas* (slaves), who were brought into the category called *jati*. The indigenous peoples who resisted the aggression of the Aryans came to be known as *Jana* and their settlements were called as *Janapada*. Of them those who fought against the invaders tooth and nail were called as 'Rakshasa' meaning cannibals, and 'Dasyu' meaning bandits. In the Brahmanical Hindu myth the headman of the Kaivartas or fisherfolk in the seacoast was known as *Mahamondalika* or Mahish and the headman of the people living in the forests was known as Asur. So the leader of the Aryan invader Durga, equipped with combined weapons of the Devatas, had to face the united opposition of the indigenous people under the leadership of Mahisasur in which Mahisasur was killed.[1] The same tradition continued later. The indigenous people were collectively addressed as *'villa'* or uncivilized during the Vaisnav period. To quote the famous lines of Krishnadas Kaviraj, the biographer of Sri Chaitanya Mahaprabhu,

> *Jharikhander Pathe Prabhu Karila Gaman*
> *Villa praya Lok-taha Param Pasanda.*
>
> Travelling through Jharikhand or Jharkhand the people are *Villa* or uncivilized and they are *Pasanda* i.e. great sinful people.

In the entire *Mangal Kavya* of the Bengali literature, the indigenes were termed as *Rarh* and *Chuar* meaning uncivilized and crude people as rightly pointed out by Dr. Kshirod Chandra Mahato in his book *Bangla Mangal Kavey Vaisnav Pravab* (2004). Moreover in *Durga Charit* it is written :

*Mundunelan hanosvanimi Kol bidhvangs nisthatha*
In the war as Indra killed the Mundas, similarly Durga killed the Kols.[2]

The Kol people, who were brought to seacoast of Haldia for the salt preparations by the Portuguese traders before the subjugation of the East India Company, were known as Malangi.[3] The term Kol means those who eat pigs and also those who are as black as pigs. The Ho, Bhumij, Kudmi, Munda and Santhal were termed as 'Kol' in that part of the country. Specially in Baleshwar and Cuttak, those people are still termed as Kolha by the dominant sections of the Oriyas. The Kurmis in Bengal are called as 'Chuars' meaning barbarians. The same attitude is visible in other parts of India. The name 'Naga' for a group of peoples in the North-Eastern part of the country means the 'Naked people'. A Sanskritized section of the great Shavaras in Orissa is called *suar* (swine ). The name 'Panias' in South India stands for slaves.

One should however know how the indigenes represent themselves. The Munda called themselves as Horoko, Santhal call themselves as Hor, while Hos address themselves as Ho, Kudmi as Kudmi-Hor, all meaning man. In Tripura the indigenous people called themselves as Borok which denotes man and their language is known today as Kol-Borok i.e. the language of man. On the other hand indigenous agriculturists and artisan communities are termed by the indigenous people in Jharkhand as Mitan of friendly people like Kamar, Kumbhar, Tanti, Chik-Boraik, Jolha, Napit, Pytkar, Rajovar,Bhuiya, Muchi, Thethri, Karga etc. Against this another very powerful but oft-used word is *Diku* who denote out-groups. They are migrants and having no social, cultural and traditional political obligation to the indigenous norms, signs, symbols including folk songs and dances including Chho, Karam, Tusu, Bandna as well as festivals and rituals.

## Assertion and Reassertion by the Jharkhandi

It is true that the indigenes were not always able to offer resistance to political as well as cultural aggressors and chose instead to recede to the safety of the hills and forests for survival and growth. History is however replete with instances when they staged stubborn resistance to the colonial onslaught of the Aryans and the Brahmanical Hindu states, Muslim and British rulers, and finally of the advanced nationalities and 'internal colonialism' of the modern Indian state. The constraint of space however allows me to narrate the story of Jharkhandi assertion during colonial rule only and to do so I shall mostly invoke the history of indigenous struggle and also suffering as depicted in the oral tradition.

It was during the initial days of the East India Company when the British were destroying the *sal* forest and exporting the *sal* woods to Europe, the Lodha Sabars of the then *Jangal Mahal* revolted against the destruction of forest. The leaders of the first forest movement Keshu Aari and Raghunath Mahato were hanged in 1763 at Keshiari near Kharagpur, West Midnapur. After a few weeks seven Lodha-Sabar leaders were hanged at Lodhasuli near Jhargram on the National Highway today. It will be interesting to note that the Lodha-Sabars and Kudmi Mahatos were early settlers in this part of the country. A song noted below recreates the saga of indigenous resistance.[4]

*Kesu Aarir Fansi hailo*
*Raghunath Mahto Bandaigelo*
*Bansbone Dom hailo Kana*
*Rage Jalchche Jangal Mahal Thana.*[5]

Kesu Aari was hanged, Raghunath Mahato was chained and hanged. In the bamboo grove, the Doms or bamboo workers became blind, the whole of Jangal Mahal was burning (against the East India Company).

It was perhaps because of the uncompromising attitude of the Lodhas that the stigma of 'criminal' and 'hostile' words were imposed on them. It may be suggested that since then the indigenous people in general came to be termed as 'tribe' which also implies 'uncivilized', arrogant and foolish people.

When the first Chuar rebellion (1765-67) started, the indigenous people specially the Kudmi, Gond, Bauri, Bhumij from Karnagarh to Jhalda and Panchkot asserted their identity in relation to *Jal, Jangal* and *Jamin*. To quell the insurgency in 1766, Graham, the Resident Commissioner, ordered Lt. Farguson to occupy *Jangal Mahal*. The rebels had their camps mainly at Chiyara, Nayabasan, Belaibera, Jhargram, Jamboni, Lalgarh, Kalyanpur, Ghatsila, Patamda and Jhalda areas. At Jhargram fort and at Radhanagar serious confrontation took place. The queen Rani Siromani of Midnapur, Malladevs of Jhargram and the rulers of Panchakot, Dhalbhumgarh, Manbajar etc. fought against the East India Company's army. The leader of the Layek or Nayak Achal Sing and leader of the Bauris-Bagdis Gobardhan Dikpati and Nimai Sardar of the Munda-Bhumij and others were hanged. The saga of their bravery formed the theme of the following folksong :

*Hansa rajar chatra sing*
*Charal achal sing*
*Eho mal bhuiye sajalo larai*
*Ganganir tyare ho, fanshi helai*
*Fanshi helai gobardhan*
*Gobardhaner sangati nimai*[6]

Achal Sing, the leader of the Chuars, revolted against white rulers and the Mallabhum was in total warpath. In the field of Gangani (Near Belpahari), Gobardhan Dikpati was hanged and his assistant Nimai Mahato was also hanged.

Interestingly the people living in Salboni, Supur, Jhargram, Dhalbhum, Phulkusma and Manbazar have forgotten those historical events. But what is interesting is that people who were forced to migrate to Dacca, Rajsahi, Dinajpur areas of Bangladesh still remember the incidents as narrated by the folk songs.

The assertion of the indigenes for their rights over *Jal, Jangal, Jamin* continued. This is amply borne out by the second Chuar rebellion (1772-1793), Kol insurrection (1831-32), Bhumij revolt (1833-34), first Santhal rebellion (1855-1856), Great Rebellion of (1857-58), second Santhal rebellion (1861), Birsa Munda's Ulgulan (1895-1899) and Meli Movement (1917-19). We learn of the traditional mobilization strategy applied by the *Majhi-pargana, Mahato-pargana*, and *Desh-Majhi* system through *Sarjom-Dharowa* (sending Sal leaves with the sound of drums) which is invitation to all the members of the ethnic groups. This was narrated in a folk song related to the first Santhal rebellion :

*Sidhu Kanu khurkhurir upare*
*Chand-Vairab lahare lahare*
*Chanku Mahato, Rama Gope Lahare lahare.*
*Challu Jolha lahare lahare*

Sidhu and Kanu are on the palanquin, Chand and Vairab are looking them along with Chanku Mahato, Rama Gope and Challu-Jolha looking them with respect.

A song on the indigo plantation in Rajsahi, Nadia and Sundarban similarly records

*Gopal Mahato bere rage*
*Lagrai pitilo khari*
*Nilchas Ultaidilo, Biswanath, Sardare he*

Gopal Mahato was a very angry man he sounded through his drums and the indigo cultivation was stopped by Biswanath Sardar.[7]

There were yet other modalities of transmission of rebel-message as depicted by a folk song during *Bhumij Hangama* or *Ganganarayani Hangama* :

*Jagannather sal gira*
*Oho lal singer Dharowa*
*Ganganarayan agu agu*

*Buli Mahator hunkari*
*Barabhum kaisan garam.*
*Oho Kaisan Gram.*

Jagannath Dhal's messages through 'Sal Gira' (through a twig of two sal leaves), Lal Singh's sound of war through drum, Ganganarayan Sing was in front, Buli Mahato's call through mouth. How is the village Barabhum?

While I was doing field work in Baghari village in Dampara hills I could collect another such folk song in 1967 :

*Awa dekha bhai dhalbhum sarag muluk*
*Damparar shyam munda singa phunklo*
*Subla singe dhol*
*Ganjan Mahato lagra bhai*
*Chale manush chalake chalake*
*Oho, Manuslo chale Bahir para*
*Oho, Sabanrekhar Bahir para.*

Oh brothers, come and see the land of Dhalbhum, it is like heaven. The *singa* (bugle) was played by Shyam Munda of Dampara and *dhol* (drum) was played by Subal Singh, and Ganjan Mahato played the *lagra*. The combined sound was a call of war, the people marched like a flow of the river stream and became a human stream like the flow of Subarnarekha river.

Indigenous movement utilized *padyatra* (collective march) to mobilize popular support and to register their protest. In Indian history the first such march perhaps had been organised during second Santhal rebellion in 1861 as a modality of subaltern protest. Under the leadership of Sundar Majhi, Jagannath Teli, Thulku Mahato (Thurua Mahato) and others 50,000 people from Dumka, Banjhi, Rajmahal marched to Suri. Later their twenty five representatives went to Calcutta to meet with Lt. Governor. Similarly second *padyatra* was organised by Birsa Munda who with ten thousands people marched from Sail Rakab forest to Ranchi, to protect their rights over *Jal, Jangal, Jamin.*[8]

It will however be pertinent to mention that not merely subaltern assertion but elite leadership of popular protest became the theme of folk song. During 1857-58, the Raja of Porahat led the popular uprising of the Ho. We find this recorded in a song.

*Sal gacher sal Ponkra*
*Kadamgacher Kalire*
*Arjun Singer lal-gamcha*
*Porahat rajar lalgamecha*
*Chatak dekhe morire*

> The Sal twigs of sal tree and the budded flowers of Kadam tree, the red coloured *gamcha* of Arjun Sing, the king of Porahat, the glamour of the king is so loving and attractive.

The last line amply bears out the reason why Arjun Singh was able to elicit the support from the people of Manbhum, Barabhum, Jhalda and Hazaribagh in the Rebellion of 1857-58.

*Chal tusu chal khelte jabo*
*Raniganjer bortola*
*Khelte khelte dekhai ainbo*
*Phansi diya gach tola*
*Oho Egaro loker phansi hailo bhai*
*Sukhdev Mahator phanci hailo bhai*
*Taher Ali bandalo,*
*Oho egaro loker phansi hailo bhai*

> Oh, Tasu let us go to play to the shadow of banian tree at Ranigunj, and during the play, I shall show you the tree where the hanging took place. Eleven persons were hanged, Sukhdev Mahato was hanged, Taher Ali was arrested (and hanged). Oh, eleven persons were hanged. [9]

Raja Nilmoni Singhdeo was the other feudal chief who provided leadership to popular movements. A Tusu song records this historic role of the Raja :

*Kolkatake gele tusu*
*Mokaddamar ki hailo*
*Mokaddamay degree koire*
*Nilmoni Bandai Gelo.*

Oh! Tusu you have visited Kolkata, but what about the Criminal Case? You know Nilmoni won the Case, but he was put under imprisonment.

In 1917-19, Mayurbhanj witnessed a serious peasant uprising known as Meli movement.[10] This uprising was a combined movement against military recruitment for the first World War. Kanka Majhi, Kalia Mahato, Retu Kol-Kumar and Nayan Sing Munda Mahato were hanged. 37 people were sentenced to life and nearly 700 people were jailed. On the basis of sources in the British India Library, K.S Singh referred this as the biggest trial in India. A Tusu song records[11]

*Bhanjabhuiye meli hailo*
*Kanka majhir phansi hailo*
*Oh tusu hamar agdahli*
*Dekhbi tora ai.*
*Kalia Mahator phanshi hailo*
*Baripada jharjhanai*
*Retu kol-kumar aur*
*Nayan Sing Munda marod bathe bhai*

Kanka Majhi was hanged but our Tusu was the leader, come and see. Kalia Mahato, Retu Kol Kamar were hanged. Nayan Sing Munda was also hanged. But you see they were all male truly.

The indigenous people of Jharkhand were subjected to deprivation by their fellow countrymen—the Oriya, Bihari, Bengali people who imported the exotic culture represented by the Grand Tradition. The inroad of Sanskritization had long past manifested in the Rajputization of several tribal chiefs. It is true that the indigenes in general had adapted elements of Hindu and Christian religions as instanced by the Sardari, Kherwar, Safa Hor, Birsite, Tana Bhagat, Bhumij—Kshatriya,

Kurmi-Kshatriya movements. Though the Notification No. 550 of 1913 by the Government of India declared all the indigenous people as 'aboriginals' to safeguard their interests, it cannot be denied that these forces were instrumental in the marginalization of the indigenes and their culture. Two instances will make my point clear.

In 1937 election, the indigenous people lost their candidates in Purulia general seat to Upendra Nath Bhattasali, Mayurbhanj seat to Khitish Chandra Niyogi and Lalmohan Patra and Jhargram-Ghatal seat to Kishori Pati Ray. Except for Lalmohan Patra and Kishori Pati Ray, rest others were from Dacca. But in Dhanbad reserved seat Tikaram Majhi was elected.

On 1 January, 1948, the Saraikela firing was initiated by the Government of Orissa only to annex Saraikela and Kharsawan to Orissa. Not less than 10,000 people were slaughtered by the Gorkha Regiment. Again on 30 January 1948 another firing by the Orissa police at Tiring and Deoposi killed several indigenous and tribal peoples.

These instances convinced the educated tribal leaders of Jharkhand region that their interests could be protected only when a separate state was created for them. Late *Marang Gomke* Jaipal Singh, late Sushil Bage, late Niral Horo, Vishnu Charan Mahato, Khudiram Mahato and Bagun Sumbrui submitted a Memorandum to the *State Reorganisation Commission* headed by Pandit Hriday Nath Kunjaru for the creation of Jharkhand. But the Central Government ignored the demand and Manbhum district was divided and a new district of Purulia was created for the settlement of refugees from East Pakistan.

Meanwhile the influx of outsiders disturbed existing demographic balance. The woe of the sons of the soil increased in subsequent decades. After the opening up of the Coal and Mica industries since the 1840s and the Iron and Steel factory at Tatanagar, Bengali, Bihari and other North Indian people immigrated in large numbers and settled in Dhanbad, Hazaribagh and Singhbhum districts. Since the inception of First Five Year Plan, the DVC as well as Bokaro, HEC Steel Plants worsened the situation further in the entire Chotanagpur plateau. It set in the most inhuman process of land alienation and displacement of those who were rooted to this soil. It will be pertinent to point out that since the Tata factory came up at Kalimati, Jamshedpur, specially the Kudmis, Bauris, Santhals, Bhumijs, Mundas, Oraons lost their lands resulting in their pauperisation. In DVC Project at Tilaiya, Konar, and Panchet not less than 213 villages were evicted mostly the indigenous people.

The suffering of the people continued. For the construction of Subarnarekha Dam at Chandil forcible eviction of villagers led to popular protest. This was retaliated by a supposed democratic government of the State of Bihar by unleashing a brutal firing on 21 October 1982 which killed two student leaders namely Ajit Mahato and Dhananjay Mahato. Moreover not less than 125 students were arrested. The leaders of the students' union who asserted their Jharkhandi identity were Ashok Oraon, Hikim Mahato and Haren Mahato. In the meantime the Bihar administration in the name of protecting reserved forest let loose a reign of terror. The Ichahatu firing (6 January1978), Kashijhore firing (7 October 1978), Surrenda firing (25 November 1978), Gua firing under the leadership of Bhaisakhu Gope (8 September 1980), Bapoiguli firing (24 November 1980), Iligara firing (4 April 1981), Tonto firing (25 April 1981), Kuira firing (26 October 1981), Kumbia firing (5 November 1981), Jajohatu firing (14 November 1981), Sarjomhatu firing (25 November 1981) etc. may be counted as tragic instances of official reprisal against those indigenous people who attempted to protect and preserve their right over *Jal*, *Jangal* and *Jamin*.

The indigenous movement was particularly marked by youth assertion. To extend the discussion further, a meeting of the Kudmi leaders of Chotanagpur and Purulia, Jhargram and Mayurbhanj was organised on 20 December 1970 at Ranchi by Jharkhand Student Association in which a joint platform of the Jharkhand movement was demanded by student leader P.K. Mahato and C.C. Mahato. On 3 January 1971, *The Hindustan Standard*, the English daily from Calcutta on the caption 'Resistances to move for descheduling and re-scheduling triabls' published the news. Lallu Oraon, Devendra Nath Champia and others formed another organization known as *Birsa Seva Dal*. Mahato informed that due to continuous pressure of the *Jharkhand Student Association* on the question of nationality and identity, *Sivaji Samaj* led by Binode Bihari Mahato, *Sanat Santhal Samaj* led by Shibu Soren and *Kamgar Union* or *Marxist Co-ordination Committee* led by A.K. Ray formed a joint confederation known as the *Jharkhand Mukti Morcha*. The entire negotiation and planning was done by the present author who was then a research scholar in Anthropology. On 9 February 1973, first Jharkhand Divas was observed and a massive rally was organised at Dhanbad. The Jharkhandi sub-nationality concept was gaining momentum. But after the murder of Nirmal Mahato, the President of *Jharkhand Mukti Morcha*, the people of Jharkhand reasserted their identity in total and in later phases when Surya Singh Besra, the leader of the AJSU, resigned from Bihar Assembly in support of separate Jharkhand state, pressure was created on the Government of India as also on the Governments of Bihar, West Bengal and Orissa. *Jharkhand Buddijibi Manch* comprising the eminent scholars and intellectuals headed by me was established. It organised two most vital national seminars at Bokaro and Jamshedpur which created a tremendous mass awareness and the leaders. Prof. Dr. B.P. Kesri, Prof. Dr. Ramdayal Munda and others also openly joined the Jharkhand movement. Finally partial Jharkhand was created on the birth day of Birsa Munda in November 2000.

It will not be out of place to mention that Jharkhandi identity has not yet been seriously asserted in Sundarban, and Nadia in West Bangal or in Bangladesh or in tea gardens of Assam and North Bengal by the labourers who had long back been forced to migrate from their birth places like Manbhum, Singhbhum, Dhalbhum, Barabhum, Sikharbhum, Khaspol, Palamau, Hazaribagh, Santhal Pargana. Dr. A.K. Sen[12] and P.P. Mahato brilliantly documented the Ho and Kudmi Santhal migration in tea gardens and Sundarban areas. The people of Jharkhand for their sympathy in Purulia in support of the coolies of Assam sung the popular song in a massive rally :

*Chal mini assam jabo*
*Dese boro dukh re*
*Assam dese re mini*
*Chah bagan Hariyal.*

> Oh, Mini (My daughter), in our land the sorrow and misery are continued but in Assam, Oh Mini, tea gardens are green.

However, everything is not green in the tea gardens today. Tea garden labourers of Assam asserted their Jharkhandi identity and demanded scheduled tribe status and marched along Guahati-Dispur streets on 29 November 2007. Unfortunately the Assamese people attacked them and a girl student was stripped naked and 21 indigenous people were killed in the riot. In protest a *bandh* was orgnaised in West Bengal, Orissa and Chhattisgarh and Bihar, the territory which in fact constitutes the geo-cultural region namely greater Jharkhand. This dream has been pithily penned by a young poet[13] in 1971-72.

*Prataya Niye bolte chai ami Jharkhandi,*
*Sal, Palas, Mahuar arale*
*Prithibir Adi-Manush ami.*

> With full of conviction I can say that I am a Jharkhandi. In the midst of Sal, Palas, Mahua trees I am the early man on earth.

Jharkhandi assertion narrated above presents the story of a fearless struggle of the people. They aspire that may all the hands get jobs, all the agricultural lands receive water for irrigation, all the villages get electricity, health and other facilities, may Jharkhandis receive modern education through their mother-tongue and not a single Jharkhandi die in starvation and hunger. Jharkhandis must aspire and endeavour for their all-round developed by asserting and reasserting their specificity as a Jharkhandi highlighting however the deprived identities of the people like Kudmi, Bhuiya, Gond, Gour, Bagal, Pan, Tanti etc.

## NOTES

1. It is interesting to know that the defeated indigenous people of Jharkhand still observed the defeat after the day of *Vijaya* and dressed like women and searched their fellow brother. The Santhals, Kudmis, Oraons, and Mundas still perform this ritual in Banjhi and Rajmahal hills and also in Panchet hills.
2. *Durga Charit*, Chapter II, p. 23. Manuscript, Sixteenth Century, The Asiatic Society, Kolkata.
3. It is a pity that the Kols who were brought as Malangi are not included in scheduled tribe list in West Bengal yet.
4. I collected the folk song which was sung by the Lodhas in a conference of the Lodhas in 1967.
5. Collected from Lukhi Sabar aged 79 on 5 April 1967 at (Lodhasuli, Jhargram). Later on I verified the information from village records, and archives of West Bengal State Government and documents of Fort William, Kolkata. The name Lodhasuli came in Jhargram area near Kharagpur. Keshu Aari, a Lodha leader along with Raghunath.
6. Collected by me from Suru Mahato on 2 September 1975 at Balurghat in West Dinajpur, Bangladesh.
7. One may come across similar such songs in the documents captioned *Zihadi Jung* (Urdu) preserved at the National Archives of Delhi.
8. Different forest acts of Government of India, debarred the indigenous people over their traditional and customary rights over the woodland. The indigenous people treated forest as their mother. Forest provided them food, fodder, fuel, fertilizer, farm implements, family housing materials, fresh air, fresh water, medicine, deities, fresh area of love, fresh and open area for hunting and hunting festival (*Disum Sendra*).
9. In this connection I would like to mention that I am one of the descendants of Sukhdev Mahato who actually hailed from Pirtanr village near Giridih. Our ancestors left the village and came to settle in Purulia, first in Bhangra and later on in village Dabar, Purulia as a cowboy or *Bagal*.
10. The Meli or united movement took place in Bhanjabhum, now Mayurbhanj in Orissa.
11. I have collected this song from Sukhi Mahato, the mother of Padmalochan Mahato of Chitorda village.
12. A.K. Sen, 'From Singhbhum to Assam : The incidence of labour emigration 1873-1918', S. Roy (ed.), *History*, Vol. II, No. I, 1999, pp. 78-88.
13. Pashuapti Prashad Mahato in SRIJAN, edited by Dr. Chittaranjan Laha, Ranchi, 1969.

**REFERENCES**


Bosu Mullick, S., (1993), *Identity Crises and Search for a New Identity.* Navdin Prakasan Kendra. ISPCK Post Box 1585, Kashmere Gate, Delhi-110006.

Mahato Pashupati Prashad, (1970), *Aami Jharkhandi (poetry)* Srijan, Ranchi Edited by C.R. Laha.

———(1982), *Jharkhand Vidhoh O Jiban,* Sujan Publication. Culcutta-29.

———(1985), *Sedin Jharkhand Rajya Holo no ken*? Sal Mahul Publication Silda, Mednipore.

———(1985), *Adivasi Arthnity O Bhumi Vaibastha.* B.B. Prakashan Calcutta-41.

———(1987), *Performing Arts of Jharkhand.* B.B. Prakasan. Calcutta-41.

———(1995), *Bharater Adivasi O Dalit Samaj,* Sujan Publication, Calcutta-41.

———(1997), *The World Views of the Santhals in Hor-Mitan and Hor-Diku* Dichotomy: A study on inter-ethnic relation in Jharkhand Social Change, March-June, Vol. 27, No. 1 and 2.

———(2000), *Sanskritization Vs Nirbakization* (A study on cultural silence and ethnic memocide in Jharkhand) Sujan Publication, Kolkata-29.

Mahato, Pashupati Prashad, (2007), Song of resistance in Jharkhand region in the book *Satyagraha as Movement*, edited by Dr. Sajal Basu. Sujan Publication. Kol-29.

Mahato, Santosh Kumar, (2002), *Munda-Parivar Adivasi Munda Samaj Jharkhand* Lapung, Ranchi, Jharkhand.

Munda, Ramdayal, (2002), *Adivasi Aastith aur Jharkhandi Asmita ke Sawal.* Prakasan Sansthan, New Delhi-2.

Munda, R.D. and S. Basu Mullick, (2003), *The Jharkhand Movement Indigenous People's Struggle for Autonomy in India.* I.W.G.I.A. Document No. 108. Copenhagen.

Padel, Felix, (1999), *The Silence of the Forest Tribes : India, Index on Censorships.* London NI 9 L.H. Fourth World Dynamics of Jharkhand.

Sengupta, Nirmal, (1982), Fourth World Dynamics of Jharkhand, Author Guild Publication, Delhi.

Mathew, S.J. Areeparampil, (2002), *Struggle for Swaraj*, Tribal Research and Training Centre (T.R.T.C.) Lupungutu, P.B-10, Chaibasa. W. Singhbhum, Jharkhand (India).

# 4

# Anti-Colonial Movements in Jharkhand and Gender Visibility

SUJATA SINGH

The integration of tribal societies of middle India with the colonial system, coupled with the influx of population from the mainland, led to many far-reaching consequences, which ultimately resulted into serious tribal movements. Along with the loss of control over land, forest and other resources, the threat to their cultural system, women being its integral part, had stirred them deeply. It remained one of focal points of all these movements. Along with other economic and political issues they made it a question of their threatened cultural identity whenever they united against the colonial powers. This particular aspect, premising the movement on cultural issue besides other, gave such movements an altogether different colour in comparison to the other northeastern tribal movements.[1]

At the same time, in spite of the fact that they had to constantly confront the incoming flow of new settlers from the mainland for various reasons, the close proximity had led to the initiation of acculturation and Sanskritisation process. It forced tribals to identify both the colonial rule and the infiltrators as potential threats to their culture, which had allowed their women folk to have a very open and free working space in the agriculture-cum-forest economy so far.[2] In fact it is true of all tribal society that women remain an integral part of the economic activities like 'cutting of timber, clearing jungles, gathering leaves and harvesting crops.' Obviously she had been enjoying a much better and comparatively freer life than their mainland counterparts. It reflected in tribal women's healthier social position. No doubt, the traditional social institution had certain limitations regarding women rights; still, it had guaranteed them a comfortable life. Notwithstanding the fact that such freedom had been soul of their culture the new settlers along with the colonial masters subjected them to ridicule and physical aggression. Since this freedom was central part of their culture, any violation was considered an assault on the very base of their pride, culture and socio-economic base. Thus, the violence against their women became one of the key issues for tribal resentment during colonial period.

However, to locate tribal women in these movements is difficult not because they are not present in the written literature, which has been a constraint in writing tribal history in general, but it becomes even more difficult when the source is either traditional tribal society or exploitative colonial rule. So the problem regarding their invisibility deepens when one has to depend on oral sources and biased official records. They provide us with very cryptic information regarding them. However, this certainly increases not only the value of those facts, which exist but the absence itself becomes conspicuous enough to be looked into.

On the other hand, since status, both ascribed and achieved, is a social position encompassing all culturally prescribed rights and duties,[3] the relevance of tribe as a social circle within which women have to work or play a role becomes very important. Consequently, besides inherited status it is the personal attainment of goals and performance over a period, which confers upon her an achieved status. It reflects in her role extension in various fields that gradually starts getting defined by the society. However the process of this kind of change is not only slow but also very complicated. The presence of strong historical forces is needed.

In the context of tribal women in Jharkhand this gradual change we do notice from nineteenth century onwards when they had to deviate from their traditional role and perform extraordinary duties during series of anti-state uprisings. It provided them with an opportunity to bring about a substantive change in their own outlook and position within the society as well. In this regard the gender participation will become more perceptible if any change in her traditional role becomes visible. The questions, therefore, arise regarding their almost non-existent presence in the contemporary chronicles. Was this invisibility due to their non-participation or issues themselves were not relevant enough to motivate them? Simultaneously, as the oral sources throw very few names in this regard the question remains what was the social attitude towards women taking part in movements basically political, violent and anti-state in nature? It is a known fact that in traditional system they hardly had any political status. So, did this negative position reflect through this attitude in any way? In such a situation could they relate with the issues involved? Moreover, any violent movement generally restricts or limits the women participation. Therefore, did this factor have any bearing on these movements where one finds excessive use of brute military strength?

The various gazetteers, reports, files etc. contain not enough facts to make suitable answers. As for example, the gazetteers especially of Santal Pargana and Hazaribagh give passing references of women during the famous uprisings of nineteenth century—the Santhal *Hul* and the *Ulgulan* of Birsa Munda. *Hazaribagh Old Record* and *1857 in Bihar* by P.C. Roychowdhury do not help much either in this context. One has to derive conclusions from the general narration of the facts with the help of the scanty references available about women. There are sufficient secondary sources available both on the tribal response to the revolt and the Santal Hul of 1855-56 i.e. K.K. Dutta's, *'The Santal Insurrection of 1855'*, *The Santal Hul* of S.P. Sinha, *the Birsa Aur Unka Andolan* of Kumar Suresh Singh etc. However, *The Elementary Aspects of Peasant Insurgency* of Ranajit Guha rather throws valuable light on the nature of women participation during Santal *Hul*. He explains her role as a member of tribal peasant society. Nevertheless, one does not find this kind of role during the Revolt of 1857. Still, the presence and absence of facts can equally be taken help of in this regard to make certain generalizations. Therefore, a distinct difference can be seen between both these anti-colonial movements against the same target groups—*mahajans, zamindar* and the state from gender point of view. However, in spite of such constraints there are enough recorded evidences of female participation, which establishes communality of *Hul* as a distinct feature of the insurrection. It got refined in coming years.

No doubt, in view of emerging questions a multi dimensional approach is essential while searching for answers. In fact, with the emergence of new and complicated situations "liable to shake the old gamut with a status"[4] such moments came with the advent of British rule in Jharkhand followed by a period of severe exploitation. The socio-economic impact had been so great that it produced a series of anti-colonial movements. However, fighting a force like British imperialism was not an easy task and required all resources of tribal energy to put in use, including women. Besides, as the events were of political nature, the consequences of excessive activities of such nature were supposed to produce results of political nature. In fact in a natural course the process of change in the context of women would have led to their taking part in decision-making process and ultimately to gender consciousness. Jharkhand having witnessed so many movements, the *Santhal Hul, Birsa Ulgulan, Tana Movement* etc., have had ample scope for such process to get begin with. So, besides looking into the traditional status, here, the contextual or contemporary factors too become very important.

That is why, the process of looking into the history of tribal women in Jharkhand, searching for an identity, requires different phases and stages of movements in this regard be reviewed keeping in mind the very nature of each stage and how did they affect women in the process. Simultaneously, the requirement is also there of doing it in the setting of their traditional status and the role they used to play in tribal world and extension being brought in with each passing phase. The pre-independent tribal movements in Jharkhand region, having women as one of its core issues, had somewhat a different approach towards them. The dominating trends may well be found in the movements of the later period as well. Most importantly, it seems, there had been a deviation from their traditional role in the society as these movements progressed from one to another in the general process of fighting the British colonialism.

The first stage came with an opportunity for such extended political role during the series of anti-colonial movements of nineteenth century. The second phase starts with the growth of nationalism, national movement and the initiation of a political process of constitutional electoral system. Jharkhand too felt the impact of mainstream struggle and consequently contributed in it, in its own way. Nonetheless, during this period the educated tribal leadership started experiencing the limitations of the national movement itself[5] as *adivasi* Christian intelligentsia was becoming aware of their distinct cultural ethnic identity and how that should be protected with the help of political rights, which were being provided by the British rulers, no doubt, with specific imperial purposes. Consequently, there started another phase of ethnic sub-national movement for autonomy came to be known as the Jharkhand movement later. But unlike the previous phase, it was remarkable for treading the path of constitutionalism and legalism and as Roy Burman has explained while making distinction between infra-nationalism and sub-nationalism, it can be said that the tribal of Jharkhand too in the first phase identified with 'tribalism'.[6] Consequently, the emergence of sub-movement during the national movement was natural. But as the demands could not be fulfilled, the movement continued through post-independence as well, with changing modality and trends.

Obviously in the presence of such strong movements of national and regional nature the issue of women cause should also have been get focused in various ways, able enough to produce consequences later on. But in reality the question of tribal women was submerged in the surge of growing Jharkhand movement gaining momentum in the wake of new political electoral process with the emergence of various regional parties, capitalizing on the growing resentment against the sub-colonial status of Jharkhand in the post-independence. For women, the newly acquired constitutional rights were considered to be enough. Thus in view of persisting problems, the exploitation of tribal women continued along with their search for solutions within and outside tribal world. To understand the 'internal process of subjugation'[7] the traditional system is needed to be analyzed as well.

Traditionally, too, in spite of the fact that in a plough culture women have no lesser rate of participation,[8] the twin issues of absolutely no representation in local traditional bodies and insufficient economic and property rights have recently been being criticized for undermining her otherwise a better status.[9] Actually, excluding certain exceptional cases, women did participate in the village assemblies or *Panchayats* but more as an aggrieved person or to give evidences. In the traditional political system of *Munda, Manki* and *Pahan* one does not find women being appointed to these posts except under special circumstances when sons were minor or there were no male children. No doubt they could take part in the meetings of general assembly but were no part of decision-making process. At best they could present their case here and had the right to be heard and ask for justice.[10] However, according to a latest theory put forward by the female activists of Jharkhand, women were not barred from such community posts and it was to crush the tribal revolts that the British not only made the post of *Parha* hereditary in place of unanimously elected one but women were said to be not entitled as well for the posts of *Manki* or *Pradhan*. The process of marginalizing women in their own society, thus, started. Though evidences are being put forward,[11] yet, more are needed to establish a general pattern, as it would weaken the theory of tribal society being a patriarchal one in Jharkhand. Actually on the basis of prevalent social norms and customary laws the tribal society in Jharkhand is said to be more patrilineal and patrilocal than exclusively a patriarchal.[12] No doubt, the long observance had provided such customs with a force of law.[13]

Nonetheless, under the impact of colonial rule an overall worsening socio-economic situation together with the weakening of traditional institutions that were responsible for maintaining social equilibrium and a safeguard against the male dominances of a patriarchal society[14], the social safety mechanisms had started somewhat losing their effectiveness to safeguard her previous advantageous position in particular cases[15]. Even historically the occurrence of instances like killing of men and women suspected of sorcery and witchcraft during 1857-58[16] shows occasional relapses on the part of traditional institution but more due to superstitious believes than anything like gender bias. The practice was a part of their belief system too. Nonetheless, one cannot deny the fact that due to simplicity of life around, the social organizations could ensure freedom and protection to its women folk, of course with certain limitations in the pre-British period. Thus, there was weakening of the system that gradually proved detrimental and giving rise to problems, which concerned women only in contemporary society. However the realization and so the reaction was simply not there.

Correspondingly, Archer's observation in this context, regarding Uraons is significant as well[17] "the principles of succession are male, the method of Government is male, the salient offices are male." But he does observe that the actual relation is one of equality, as they dance, work and live together. However, according to him a stress could be found there between the formal structure of tribal life and actual feelings and emotions of women. This kind of stress one can find in customs like hunt by women[18] or *Jani Shikar*, when they used to dress and behave like men. By behaving like a male for a single day the balance was righted. The female resentment of this seemingly patriarchal system, whatever was, thus neutralized. "The importance of the women's hunt is that through simple symbolism, the tribe keeps its balances."[19]

In fact, in tribal tales and folklores this very custom of *Jani Shikar*, when women dress and behave like men, is associated with an incident about *Uraon* women who had protected the Rohtasgarh fort thrice in garb of soldiers, some four hundred years ago against the Turks, in absence of their men. Two brave ladies, Singi Dai and Kaili Dai, are still being remembered during *Sarhul* festival.[20] These types of examples of bravery in tribal oral history and culture of pre-colonial period provided women with much needed inspiration during the anti-colonial movements. Obviously, such British observations cannot be taken for a widespread and deep resentment of women against the existing political social system rather willingness and relatively a readiness to be a part of it were certainly there. The moment came with the initiation of British rule and consequent exploitation, manifesting in the anti-colonial movements.

The very nature of anti-colonial movements asked for a greater and active role for women, different from traditional role of daily labour. Although, according to secondary sources women are visible in the insurgency of 1781-84 when they took part in guerrilla warfare,[21] yet, a definite pattern could become visible only during the insurrection of 1855-56 or *Santhal Hul*. The available official sources reflect a multi-dimensional role of them i.e. the report of civil surgeon and magistrate of Beerbhum jail regarding the medical condition of Santal women prisoners, the letter to the Secretary to the Government of Bengal, 18 July 1855 etc.[22] throw light on the kind of activities they were involved with. In fact, the effort of each member of tribal populace was needed against the mighty British Empire. Thus right from the time of organizing for the insurrection one finds women playing a role. In fact to camouflage the British suspicion, besides holding several secret meetings the help of local prevalent rituals were also taken, especially to generate the community feeling. Evidences inform us regarding one such frequently observed practice when women who were having the same number of children used to meet, dine and exchange gifts. There had been an increase in the practice. Guha calls it 'ritualisation of political process.[23]

Simultaneously, Santhal folklores are full of praise for women like Phoolo and Jhano who, it is said, had killed twenty-one soldiers.[24] Apart from that, they were not only active members of the raiding party but had to perform womanly task as well like arranging for the safety of their houses and children when males were busy fighting enemies. Besides, the entire women population has been claimed of acting as informers and providers for their men folk,[25] daring and bearing the British torture. The judicial proceedings mention the names of two women Radha and Heera, who received serious injuries while accompanying such raiding party.[26] Likewise, it is an officially known fact that the long confinements of many women in jail had made their condition pathetic especially of small children who had to accompany their mother and were dying of unhygienic conditions.[27]

The punishment pattern exhibits not only government's determination to deal with the uprising at every level but at the same time, the punishment conferred also show signs of intense involvement of women. Convicts were from as younger age group as ten to fourteen. Offences were put in the category of crime and consequently were termed sentences of rigorous imprisonment from six to three years in jail.[28]

In fact, the example of one of such imprisoned Santhal rebel family along with his wife and two daughters,[29] not only show the social impact and reach of movement and the level of commitment to the cause but grievances of an entire peasant society as well. It is true that the physical abuse of women had been a major cause of resentment[30], however, there was other issues as well which concerned women. The invisibility of women during the 1857 had much to do with the motivational strength of the issues for women. They could not relate with the issues so wide ranging-feudal, sepoy, and peasant. On the other hand, during *Hul* the entire population could well have identified with and related to the issue. The identification strengthened the movement in return.

Moreover, it is said that during raids, they involved in gathering the loot similar to "standard division of labour between the sexes at harvest time."[31] It was a type of approach, which was familiar and easy to follow for females. According to the official records they were accused and consequently convicted of 'having actively assisted' the rebel. Even those who were not such active participants and were detained of supplying provisions or spying only were not to be released unless normalcy returned to the area and they give up their old objectionable practices.[32] In fact that is why, this particular group structure of raiding party—women carrying large empty baskets for collecting loot and branch of *sal* tree and accompanying the armed group of men had become definite symbolic signs of approaching disturbances in post-*Hul* period. British knew by now that women never accompany men to *shikar* rather welcome them on their return at home.[33]

No doubt, the limited involvement of women, natural feature of a violent movement had kept it exclusively a male affair but actually even the limited involvement of women in this movement or in other words the "communality of movement" exhibited their versatile role and consequently, provided it with the status of a rebellion than only of a hunt. However, this did not mean in any way the extended political role leading to an enhanced position than before. Their rights remained the same and so the status. One even finds instances of crimes like witch hunting continued. It is also said that during and just after the *Hul* the political and social surroundings of tribal world had become more male dominated.[34] Still, the trend could not take deep roots. In fact the recent researches explain this development as occasional one when the local people taking advantage of the weakening of British power had tried to resist the imperial authority through disobeying its instruction of checking the practice of witchcraft.[35]

However, there is no doubt about the fact that the base of tribal society—collective action or community participation was certainly there. In addition, the realization on the part of women of nexus between the state and the local feudal element that used to take away her cheap iron ornaments at times developed.[36] In spite of the instruction of the commissioner of Bhagalpur regarding families of rebels be spared as 'British government does not make war against women and children'.[37] The excessive use of state power against them further discredited the authority. In the next phase of struggle, that was during the Birsa Movement it created great confusion among the bureaucratic hierarchy as how to deal with this growing problem of women presence.

The last but most important uprising of the nineteenth century further refined this realization. Even from the gender point of view there occurred an important change. Unlike Santhal *Hool,* the Birsa Movement of 1900 while resisting the colonial power aimed at reviving the ancient golden age of Mundas[38] and in this regard one of his visions of an ideal society was where there was no violence against women. Simultaneously, by advising tribal men to practice monogamy and suggesting equal moral rules for both the sexes he did try to purify the male attitude.[39] However, in spite of women issue being one of the important components of his revivalist programmes the efforts were more directed to keep the society from degrading further than for the sake of women emancipation. He was more concerned with restoring the former glory of Mundas and according to some opinion emulating the practice of Hindu and Christian society. The issue of exploitation of women remained more a matter of tribal honour. This type of Birsa's programmes certainly sought for and had scope for appeal to the tribal men only.[40] In fact the articulation of the whole issue was rather to enhance the position of society by encouraging tribal men to abstain from certain evils than to encourage women themselves to take up any such issues.

The patriarchal structure tends to limit the role of women in resisting the anti-women actions themselves. Since there was no change in it so like previous movements their role remained still confine to, being a participant only. It hardly had any scope for the growth of leadership quality, which ultimately would have enhanced their political position within the movement and in the society both. Still, the overall approach had positive results on their position in the movement. There had been a gradual but obvious extension in the nature of participation and they started taking more active part in raids and guerrilla war[41] as regular combats quite frequently, which immensely strengthened these movements.

In fact in both the decisive encounters of Birsa Movement—Sail Rakab and Etkedih women were present.

From the little information available, the image one gets regarding their role is certainly of a spirited fighter who could fight quite easily with deadly traditional weapons with which she was used to work in dangerous surroundings—forests and fields. Thus, weapon had become a regular feature of her life not only because of personal safety but sometimes even agricultural tools too served the purpose of deadly weapons, especially axe, with which she used to cut or clear woods for fuel and more agricultural lands. No doubt, both this kind of acquaintance or use of such weapons and dangerous working condition had imbibed a unique fighting spirit in them. The factual report of Deputy Commissioner Mr. Streetfield had mentioned about encounter at Etkedih during Birsa Movement when Maki the wife of one of the prominent tribal leaders Gaya Munda and his two daughters-in-law had fought with weapons like 'lathi', 'tangi' and 'dauli'. Likewise, there are references of his three daughters Thigi, Nagi and Lembu fighting vigorously with weapons like sword, axe and 'tangi' till their weapons were snatched and they were overpowered. They had to fight while holding their kids in one hand and weapons with another.[42] According to Streetfield, Maki was an old but ferocious lady who had injured the Daroga Altaf Hussein by throwing an axe towards him. He further describes those women in adjectives like ferocious, stubborn, and mad and in the same way brave also. This kind of spirit had made Deputy Commissioner very apprehensive regarding other women.[43]

The visible evidence of active women participation at Sail Rakab was the turning point regarding the British thinking about the seriousness of the situation. It produced reactionary responses. In fact, the British soldiers got so annoyed that they kept shooting at even fleeing rebels including women against the order of Forbes for shooting only in self-defence. Three women, wives of Bankan Munda, Majhia Munda, and Dungdung Munda of Jiuri, were shot dead.[44] It made a ruckus at higher echelon of British bureaucracy. There were explanations to be sought. The officials had to justify their actions by saying that both men and women were having long hairs so it had become difficult for them to make a difference from a distance. Nevertheless, the Government of India criticized the civil and army officials both in soft words for the unfortunate death of these women.[45] In fact the incident had formed a serious situation for them. The excessive use of armed strength had created a feeling of deep distrust, which might have turned into a mass movement. In such a situation indication of women taking part was a matter of great concern.

However, even after the massacre of Sail Rakab followed by large scale arrests rebel women kept persuading others to join the uprising.[46] The incident at Sail Rakab did not deter the strong resolve of Birsa's follower and their wives.[47] It can be corroborated by another reference of Birsa Movement which mentions two rebel tribal women, Champi and Sali, as among the most trusted ones and when a reward of Rs. 500 was announced to person who would catch Birsa, they remained with him till the end.

Moreover, the symbolic significance of hunt was again there. After the encounter at Sako under the leadership of Gaya Munda who killed one constable, women washed the feet of men on their return as was the custom and men sang the *shikar* songs.[48] The point, knows fully well the consequences of being a part of such violent movement, tribal women were ready for the kind of active armed participation and sacrifice the movements were asking for. Consequently, they could easily extend their role and become part of these armed resistance.

The two years of rigorous imprisonment to Maki and jail to her daughters and daughters-in-law were severe and shows the realization of the gravity of situation on the part of British authority.[49] Actually it was this kind of active participation, which made Streetfield apprehensive of other tribal women, too, having the same kind of vigour and courage.[50] The theory that the participation of women makes any movement visible and consequently raises its standard seems here worth taking note of.

In spite of such role extension the gender and political consciousness on the part of women themselves and the local power structure could not be developed so much to use this understanding further in the actions of twentieth century modern movements. Contrarily, in other parts of contemporary India one finds presence of both national and women movements, giving evidences of such historical forces. Actually in Jharkhand, which had been subjecting to grievous economic exploitation, the process took a different course when the need for preserving tribal identity in the changing political context encouraged people to demand autonomy in the twentieth century. The bifurcation of Bihar and Orissa in 1936 further kindled their hopes. In 1938, the political party of Adivasi Mahasabha came into existence with twin objectives of a separate state of Jharkhand and protection of Adivasis against exploitation. Obviously, this kind of movement had an ethnic tenor and potential to dilute the national feeling in the twentieth century.

Still, women did become part of this sub-national and regional movement as well. The initiation of this type of involvement tends to establish a link between general issues and issues concerning women alone, later on. Consequently, the gender consciousness develops. Therefore, the politicization of women through participation in anti-colonial movements makes it pertinent to see whether there could develop any consciousness or any linkage between the women issue and the general issue of the society and the political system. However, in absence of any women movement, organizations and their participation in the national movement comprising all sections of the society, it was the anti-colonial movements of nineteenth century and the Jharkhand movement where one could see the beginning of politicization of women in a set direction where they were more concerned about their tribal identity and interests.

In fact, the feeling got so deep rooted that it manifested in other ways. Unlike anti-colonial violent movements, the Jharkhand movement by following the peaceful constitutional methodology including electoral process encouraged and ensured women participation comparatively in significant numbers. Simultaneously the appeal of ethnic demand for them had strength too, which was expressed by the high voting percentage of women in spite of their illiteracy and lack of political training in the first general elections of free India. They made sure that their ballots had the JMM's symbol, a party championing the ethnic cause, before casting their votes. Though they lost interest later on due to political opportunism and factionalism.[51]

Nonetheless, these instances show how women had been taking part in those movements and particularly on the issues that did not directly concern her but at the same time it was very natural for them to identify with the more fundamental issues like colonial exploitation. There had to be a starting point to move to some more specific issues like witch hunting, drinking habit of males, problems of women labourers working in mines, kiln etc. In the meanwhile the condition of women remained stagnant. The preoccupancy of tribal leadership elsewhere all through the twentieth century led to the piling up of problems, which concerned women only.

Obviously there had not been any dearth of issues. She had not only been victim of colonial exploitation but at the same time some inherent fundamental problems were also there in the traditional system. However, in spite of having problems emerging out of land alienation, agriculture still remained a major area of economic activities and employment for females. It was here that she was to play a particular role with the help of traditional rights and be worthy of the status given to her by the society. The gap between the roles she had been playing since ages and the status given to her by the society in view of fast changing socio-economic scenario could well determine her position in the society. Since the colonial rule had already initiated certain process affecting tribal life, consequently the deviation from the traditionally accepted economic-social role by becoming labourer in mines, construction work, plantations etc. and migrating to far off places led to her losing the social status within the tribal society as well.[52] In Jharkhand, no doubt, women had been in the centre of all economic and social activities but going by the economic rights she had, which would have complimented her role, her status remained more of a cooperator. As for example the system of male inheritance prevalent among the major tribes in Jharkhand has somewhat affected her by making her position, economically weak, dependent and insecure.[53] Later on, it was argued keeping in mind her involvement in agriculture that she should be enjoying the rights of a primary cultivator[54] or in other words by this way she was to be put in altogether a different class—agriculturist. Besides, there existed certain taboos restricting her free movement in certain essential areas of agricultural production.[55] The point is, certain inherent disadvantages were there in the traditional system itself having the potential of turning into an issue. Here she was at par with rest of the women. But she was at a disadvantage because by being the part of national movement she could have become more aware of their specific interests, issues, need for an organization and consequently an able leadership could have emerged through participation as had happened during anti Parda movement in Bihar during the National Movement. A very few number of women leaders, who are visible in written documents, did emerge but they were directly related to the male leaders of the movements. It seems it provided a sort of acceptability to their leadership in the tribal society. The very trend becomes relevant when it followed through the post-independence or led to the emergence of a political elite class later on.

No doubt this kind of political consciousness is necessary to ask questions about the nature of participation or to whose interests it is being directed.[56] However, the absence of more enlightened involvement or in other words the lower level of participation during the first-half of twentieth century was to produce significant results later on when important changes, which were being made in the electoral process in India before the general elections of 1930s. Yet, the reasons for the low percentage of women voting were attributed to *parda*, Congress boycott and a general lack of interest in electioneering. In case of tribal women the last one applies. Likewise the representation given to different sections including two to Adivasi candidates in 1920 and the reservation of seven seats in Bihar legislative assembly under the Act of 1935 could hardly help them raise the level of political awareness, as she was still to become a part of that process. Her political status was still non-existent.

On the other hand the series of anti-colonial struggle of the nineteenth century did help them in developing an ethnic consciousness, which was later used by the regional political parties in electoral politics as well. Since majority of women belonged to rural areas, so it was here the colonial feudal alliance induced oppression was felt the most and as the women participation increased in anti-colonial movements, there had been a slow growth of consciousness about ethnic identity among them. Actually, one of the results of the colonial rule was the emergence of feudal element and tendencies in the tribal life.[57]

This addition of feudalistic element in the patriarchal society of tribal in Jharkhand further complicated the situation for women within and outside the society as well. Still, one finds her presence in the movements being organized against such element. One name of Deomani Bandhani may be mentioned who kept the movement against the *zamindars* alive by providing an effective leadership when Jatra Bhagat was arrested in 1914. Several tribal became Tana followers under the leadership of Deomani.[58]

As said above, this deep resentment against the colonial rule had the potential of being used by the vested parties for their sub-national demand for separate state with which the tribal women could easily relate to than the national demand. Consequently the fundamental issues for women, as has been discussed above, could not get as much attention as was required, during the colonial and post-independent period too, when she got the constitutional rights. Not the least the awareness to have an organization could also grow much later[59] as it happens only when groups of like minded people, having similar interests starts feeling the same way. Even by being associated with the issue like the Jharkhand movement she strengthened the present pattern of development rather than directing this pattern to her own development. Even the political agenda of various parties again advocated the activization of same old traditional institutions which certainly did not mean meaningful participation in the decision-making process.[60]

However, such all-round consciousness is linked with the growth of education and politicization, which leads to the growth of intellectual level of the group itself.[61] Only then the new pressure can be built upon the original sub-national or ethnic identity, which becomes answerable in the process to the group. In Jharkhand the process to ask such questions could start much later in the post-independence period.

The presence of women in any movement on issues—general and personal—makes that movement visible and publicized besides strengthening it. The growing participation of tribal women in each anti-colonial movement demonstrated the gravity of situation to British authorities in clear terms. Apart from economic consequences the social impact of their rule, supported and aided by the feudal element, was well gauged by, due to female resistance.

It has been suggested that in a country with colonial linkage women get liberating ideas with the generation of anti-colonial, anti-feudal struggles and not with the development of capitalism.[62] Again it is viewed that liberation is a process in which women with private interests raised to a level of women with public interests and activities.[63] The application of first one is right in the context of Jharkhand; the reverse of the second one is true. Women got involved in the process of restructuring the superstructure through becoming part of various anti-colonial, constitutional and sub-national movements first. Then only the process to remove the ills affecting her social status within the family and the society could get start. Likewise, the prerequisite conditions essential for such change i.e. an organization, an effective leadership, gender consciousness; quality participation in movements based only on relevant women issues etc. also started becoming visible.

The studies regarding genesis and evolution of women's movement in modern India have led to many assumptions. One of those considers the discourses of nationalism, secularism and democratic liberalism as western categories, still, which have much to offer to Indian women. Nonetheless, once reconstructed they do not necessarily remain the prisoner of construct and it is only the course of events, which may lead to redefinition of goals and strategies as need may be. The application of this assumption in the case of tribal women's movement in Jharkhand leads us to some healthy but certain alarming emerging trends as well needed to be understood in right direction and perspective.

## NOTES & REFERENCES

1. K.S. Singh (ed.), *Tribal Movements in India,* Vol. I, Manohar, 1982, pp. IX-X.
2. K.K. Dutta, *The Comprehensive History of Bihar,* Vol. III, Part II, K.P. Jayaswal Research Institute, Patna, 1976, p. 303.
3. K. Mann, *Theoretical Orientation Tribal Women in a Changing Society,* New Delhi, 1987, p. 8.
4. *Ibid.,* p. 14.
5. Mathew Areeparampil, *Struggle for Swaraj,* Tribal Research and Training Centre, 2002, Jamshedpur, p. 231.
6. K.S. Singh (ed.), *Tribal Movements,* p. 19.
7. Vidyut Bhagvat, *Feminist Social Thought,* Rawat Publications, Jaipur and Delhi, 2004, p. 327.
8. K.S. Singh, Tribal Women and Their Land Rights in our Tribal Heritage, The National Tribal Festival, 1989, p. 61.
9. Appraisal Report, *Bihar-Madhya Pradesh Tribal Development Programme,* Vol. II, Govt. of India, 1999, p. 16 (Annexure-1).
10. A.C. Mittal and J.R. Sharma (eds.), *The Tribal Women in India,* Radha Publication, New Delhi, 1998, p. 187.
11. Vasvi, Ulgulan ki Mahilayen, Harivansh (ed.), *Disum Muktigatha aur Srijan Ke Sapne,* Rajkamal Prakashan, New Delhi, 2002, p. 146.
12. Mittal & Sharma, *The Tribal Women,* p. 195.
13. Verrier Elvin, *A New Deal for Tribal India,* Ministry of Home Affairs, New Delhi, 1962, p. 129.
14. K.K. Dutta, *op cit.,* The Comprehensive History, pp. 324-328.
15. Appraisal Report, pp. 14-15.
16. L.S.S. O'Malley (ed.), *Modern India and the West : A Study of the Interaction of Their Civilization,* Oxford University Press, 1941, p. 734; Dalton, E.T., *Descriptive Ethnology of Bengal,* Govt. of Bengal, Calcutta, 1872, p. 208.
17. Verrier Elwin, *Tribal Women,* in Tara Ali Beg (Ed.), *Women of India,* Publications Division, 1958, p. 209.

18. *Ibid*, p. 211.
19. *Ibid.*
20. Vasvi Ulgulan, p. 145.
21. Mathew Areeparampil, Struggle for Swaraj, p. 66.
22. Chaturbhuj Sahu, *The Santal Women*, Sarup & Sons, New Delhi, 1996, pp. 165-170.
23. Ranjit Guha, *Elementary Aspects of Peasant Insurgency in Colonial India*, Oxford University Press, New Delhi, 1983, p. 266.
24. *Ibid.*
25. JP No. 97, from Offig. Magistrate of Beerbhum K. Thompson to A.N. Russel Under Secretary to the Govt. of Bengal, Judicial Department, Fort William regarding sanitary condition of the female ward of Jail where 20 Santhal women awaiting trial; Appendix-2(C), Chaturbhuj Sahu, *The Santhal*, p. 165; Guha, Elementary Aspects, p. 132; Mathew Areeparampil, Struggle for Swaraj, p. 155.
26. *Ibid.*, p. 130.
27. JP No. 97, *op. cit.*, p. 165.
28. *Ibid.*
29. Guha, Elementary Aspects, p. 131.
30. The extension of two hundred miles of railway line skirting the Santal country created a demand for cheap labour which definitely included women and nevertheless, subjected them to the ill designs of railway staffs. R.R. Diwakar, Bihar through the Ages, Orient Longman, Delhi, p. 600 (also see Mittal and Sharma, K.K. Dutta, The comprehensive, p. 95).
31. Mittal and Sharma, *op. cit.*, p. 188.
32. Chaturbhuj Sahu, *op. cit.*, p. 166.
33. P.C. Roychowdhury, Hazaribagh Old Records, Revenue Department, Government of Bihar, Patna, 1957, p. 40.
34. Nabendu Datta-Majumdar, *The Santal: A Study in Culture Change*, Government of India Press, Calcutta, 1956, p. 37.
35. Sabyasachi Bhattacharya (ed.), Rethinking 1857, Sasank Shekhar Sinha, on the margines of a National Uprising: The Dynamics of 1857 in Chotanagpur, Orient Longman, New Delhi 2007, pp. 136-37.
36. P.C. Roychowdhury, *op. cit.*, p. 189.
37. K.K. Dutta, The comprehensive, pp. 29-30.
38. Mittal and Sharma, The Tribal, p. 191.
39. *Ibid.*, pp. 189-190.
40. *Ibid.*, p. 191.
41. Mathew, Struggle for Swaraj, p. 66.
42. Kumar Suresh Singh, *Birsa Munda Aur Unka Andolan*, Classical Publications, New Delhi, 1979, pp. 112-113.

43. Kumar Suresh Singh, *Birsa Munda Aur Unka Andolan,* Classical Publications, New Delhi, 1979, pp. 112-113.
44. *Ibid.*, p. 235.
45. *Ibid.*, p. 124.
46. *Ibid.*, p. 136.
47. *Ibid.*, p. 127.
48. *Ibid.*, p. 111.
49. Vasvi, Ulgulan, p. 153.
50. *Ibid.*, pp. 151-152.
51. D.D. Guru, *Jharkhand Movement : Need for Emphasis on Education and Socio-Economic Development of the Region,* in Jharkhand Movement Origin and Evolution, Inter-India Publication, New Delhi, 1992, p. 133.
52. L.S.S. O'Malley (ed.), Modern India, p. 415.
53. Sulbha Brahma, *Effects of Mobilization on Women's World View,* Shankar Brahma Samajvidryna Granthalaya, Pune, 1983, p. 190.
54. V. Das, *Jharkhand: Castle Over the Graves,* Inter-India Publication, New Delhi, 1992, p. 79.
55. *Ibid*, p. 76.
56. Susheela Kaushik, (ed.), *Women's Participation in Politics,* Vikas Publishing House, 1993, p. xiii.
57. Dr. Gopa Joshi, *Bharat Mein Stree Asamanta, Hindi Madhyam Karyanvaya Nideshalaya,* Delhi University, 2006, p. 144.
58. Vasvi, Ulgulan, p. 147.
59. Mittal and Sharma, The Tribal Women, p. 196.
60. *Ibid.*, p. 195.
61. Amartya Sen, *The Argumentative Indian,* Penguin Books, 2006, pp. 221-222.
62. M. Bhatia, *History and Social Change in India,* New Delhi, p. 70.
63. *Ibid.*

# 5

# Zamindars, Christian Missionaries and Tribals of Chotanagpur on the eve of *Sardari Larai*

CHITTARANJAN KUMAR PATY

Chotanagpur was the abode of the Munda, Oraon, Santhal, Ho and Kharia tribals who had their own mode of life since ancient times. Some socio-economic and political changes during both pre-colonial and colonial times adversely affected the peaceful existence of these indigenous people which brought the whole area in ferment. Nineteenth century Chotanagpur thus became the period of upheavals in the history of Chotanagpur when several revolts occurred in this area.

Before the advent of British rule in the eighteenth century A.D., some political kingdoms like Cheros of Palamau, Nagbanshis of Chotanagpur khas (Ranchi) and Singh dynasties of Singhbhum had been established. With the formation of all these dynasties, there arose a powerful group of *zamindars* and *jagirdars* in the area.[1] Like the medieval knights, they had their own soldiers which were used against these tribals. The indigenous people were forced to work in their fields and provide every thing for them. The *Calcutta Review* of July 1869 describes the horrible picture of the society.[2] These *rajas* and *zamindars* invited the Hindu and Muslim courtiers such as priests, clerks and servants for their daily works.[3] Thus many Hindus and Muslims entered this region as courtiers of these Houses.

Later during British rule the process of the immigration of outsiders accelerated with the appointment of large number of Biharis and Bengalis *amlahs.* All these non-tribal people changed the socio-political life of the region. They began to exploit the indigenous populace. They collect many taxes from the tribals such as Gunahgari, Salami, opium tax and taxes from Daks also. Sometimes they forcibly took the goat or oxen for sacrifices. In fact they extorted bribes from the tribals.[4] As the tribals disliked them, they called these new comers *dikus* (trouble-makers) and since then, the term *dikus* was used for non-tribals people by these native people.[5]

The exploitation of the non-tribals was so extreme that this led to a gigantic uprising which is known as Kol Insurrection of Chotanagpur in 1831-32. Then Harnath Sahi, the brother of Jagannath Sahi, Mahraja of Chotanagpur, made grants of villages in Sonapur Pargana to some of the Sikhs and Muslims. The land which were given to the outsiders originally belonged to the indigenous people. Most of the Mankis and Mundas were the hereditary proprietors of the land. Now they had been dispossessed of their lands by transferring these to the foreigners whom they disliked.[6] In this new arrangement Singrai Manki of Bandgoan had to lose his twelve villages. This is not the one case. They dishonoured two sisters of Manki and wife of Surga Munda. These incidents enraged the whole area. Very soon, all the tribals revolted against the non-tribals. These tribals now began to butcher all the non-tribals of the villages.[7]

However, the revolt was crushed by the British Government. But the exploitation of the *zamindars* continued. The *zamindars* extorted bribes protected cattle theft, charged whole villages with dacoity and threw innocent inhabitants into jail.[8] This was not the end. During this Kol insurrection, many tribals who had abandoned the country returned in subsequent years, but as they had acted the parts of incendiaries and insurgents, the Thikadars and proprietors refused to give them back their lands. They lodged false complaints against them which forced these indigenous people to leave the villages.[9]

During this crucial time, Christianity entered Chotanagpur which brought some major changes among the *adivasis*. Four German missionaries of Berlin named Emile Schatz, August Brandt, Fredrick Batsch and Theodor Janke reached Ranchi on 2 November 1845. In Ranchi they first pitched a tent for their living. Later they got 30 acres of lands from the Maharaja of Chotanagpur and founded a mission station at Ranchi on 1 December 1845 at a place which they named Bethseda, meaning "the house of piety".[10] At present it is popularly known by the same name in G.E.L Church Compound in Ranchi. With the arrival of these missionaries Christianity spread among people. In the beginning, the converts were mostly Mundas and Oraons. Later on, other tribals also accepted Christian faith.[11] In due course many churches and schools were opened. The first church was established at Ranchi on 25 December 1845 which was known as Christ Church Ranchi. Later on several other churches came into existence. Their main centre of activities were Ranchi, Gobindpur, Lohardaga, Murhu, Itki, Sarwada, Maranghada, Ramtolya, Chaibasa, Hazaribagh and other places of Chotanagpur.[12]

With the preachings the number of tribal Christians increased day by day and by 1857 their number was about 800 in Chottanagpur.[13] The missionaries of Chotanagpur besides proselytising the people were mainly responsible to a great extent for the dawn of education. The first school was founded in 1852 which was named as Bethseda School in Ranchi. In 1856 Gossnar High School was founded in Ranchi.[14] Later on, many other schools were opened in other missionary centres of Chotanagpur. Through their educational institutions rays of western influence poured forth. The school attracted the aboriginal people. Both children and adults used to go to schools where they had been taught by foreign teachers. Not only that, the students were encouraged to come regularly by paying one anna per week from the schools also. All these encouraged these indigenous people.[15]

During the time of mutiny besides the *rajas* and *zamindars* there were about six hundred *jagirdars* in Chotanagpur and each *jagirdar* held between one and 150 villages in their possession.[16] But in fact the *rajas* and *jagirdars* had never been recognized by the Company Government. With the coming of the British in Chotanagpur the power and position of these rulers and *zamindars* slowly weakened as the British tightened theirs noose on them. Some of the dynasties which had ruled for thousand years became their subordinate and one by one subjugated by the Company Government. The rulers of Singhbhum had not even forgotten the forceful entry of the British within last twenty years and creation of a separate Kolhan from the portion of their area. The curtailment of the executive and police powers of Nagbanshi rulers created disaffection among them. Similarly Raja Churaman Rai, the last Chero King of Palamau was thrown out of the throne by the British due to non-payment of dues which angered the *zamindars* of Palamau also. [17]

Similarly, local *zamindars* of these regions were also dissatisfied with the British. As the *zamindars* usually helped for supplying troops to the *rajas* during wars so *rajas* donated lands and *jagirs* to these landlords. But after the establishment of the British power these special rights came to an end. Some of them had mortgaged their lands also and now they wanted to recapture their lost property. But this was not possible during the rule of Company Government. Due to all these economic reasons the *zamindars* were unhappy and restless.[18]

During this precarious condition of Chotanagpur the establishment of church and opening of schools made some changes here. By getting education these indigenous people realised their present position and their rights and privileges.[19] This made the converts conscious against exploitation and deprivation of their rights and privileges as original clearers of the soil, rights for which they had asserted.[20] They particularly disliked *begari* (forced labour) system which the indigenous people were forced to render to their landlords. The contact and support of the Christian missionaries so emboldened them that they henceforth refused to do forced labour in their fields. This caused a shortage of labour for cultivation which turned *zamindars* against the Christian converts.[21] On the other hand, the missionaries thought that the condition of these depressed indigenous people should be improved.[22] As the missionaries helped them against the oppressors, so the *zamindars* wanted to drive out the missionaries. They held a meeting in which they decided to stop the growth of Christianity and the missionaries. Some of the *zamindars* and their followers attacked 30 villages where Christian converts lived.[23] In this way the *jagirdars* became anti-missionaries as well as anti-British. This became one of the causes that led to the outbreak of the mutiny.

The sepoy mutiny first broke out in Meerut on 10 May 1857 and after that, it spread all over the country. Very soon Chotanagpur was also influenced by this revolt. During this time there were four main military stations in Chotanagpur—Hazaribagh, Doranda (Ranchi), Chaibasa and Purulia. When the news came to Hazaribagh that the sepoys of Danapur had risen in revolt against the British on July 25, 1857, the sepoys of Hazaribagh also revolted against the British on 30 July, 1857. They broke down the jail, looted the treasury, burned the English bungalows, *cutchery* and Bazar in Hazaribagh. After that they proceeded towards Ranchi. This alarmed the British officers and many of them including Major Simpson, Principal Assistant, Hazaribagh fled away to Calcutta with their families. Lt. Graham of Doranda Battalion was ordered by Commissioner Dalton to proceed to Hazaribagh with two companies of Ramgarh infantry to disarm the sepoys of Hazaribagh. Lt. Graham proceeded to Hazaribagh but when the sepoys reached Ramgarh, the soldiers of this battalion after hearing the news of revolt of sepoys of Hazaribagh also revolted against the British under the leadership of Jamadar Madhav Singh and Subedar Nadir Ali Khan. With some faithful soldiers, Lt. Graham managed to reach Hazaribagh on 2nd August, 1857.[24]

After hearing this news of disloyalty of the troops, Captain Dalton and other officers at Ranchi decided to vacat Ranchi. They left for Hazaribagh *via* Pithoria because they wanted to avoid the confrontation with the disloyal rebel troops which might return from Ramgarh Ranchi Road. The Parganait Jagat Pal Singh of Pithoria helped them reach Hazaribagh safely.[25] After reaching Hazaribagh on 3 August, Dalton found that the rebel sepoys had not contacted the *zamindars*. So he decided to get cooperation of the *rajas* and *zamindars*. He also sent a letter to Captain Sissmore, Principal Assistant Commissioner who was posted at Chaibasa to get cooperation from the local *rajas* and *zamindars* from Singhbhum. With the help of *Raja* of Ramgarh, Dalton was able to restore peace in Hazaribagh.[26]

Doranda rebels while returning from Ramgarh to Ranchi met with the rebel sepoys of Hazaribagh at Burmu.[27] The rebels then reached Ranchi on 2nd August under the command of Madhav Singh and Sheikh Nadir Ali Khan. On reaching Doranda (Ranchi) the sepoys of that place joined them under the leadership of Jai Mangal Pandey.[28] In the existing situation the whole of Chotanagpur khas (Ranchi) was in complete anarchy. All the businessmen of the town left Bazar. The *cutchery* of Ranchi was burnt down and the English officer's bungalows were also ransacked. Government schools were also attacked. The treasury was looted and the prisoners were released after breaking the jail. Not only that they had tried to demolish the church and attacked the G.E.L. Church Ranchi. The rebels fired four cannons on the Church and one of them hit this tower which is still visible.[29] The Christians of the mission campus were also persecuted.[30] Thus the whole of Ranchi and Doranda came under the control of the rebels.

During the mutiny local people of Ranchi had not fully supported the mutineers.[31] In this new situation, the rebel leaders very soon realised that, without the support of local *zamindars* they would not sustain the uprising in Chotanagpur.[32] So they first approached the Maharaja of Chotanagpur and his relatives but they were not ready to take leadership.[33] Ultimately, they contacted two local *zamindars* who were ready to cooperate with them. They were Thakur Biswanath Shahdeo of Barkagarh and Pandey Ganpat Rai of Bhaunro, the ex-Diwan of Maharaja of Chotanagpur.[34] Thakur Biswanath Shahdeo was already an anti-Britisher as well as anti-missionaries. The reason behind this was that the selection of civil headquarters at Ranchi and military headquarters of the Ramgarh Battalion at Doranda was made by Wilkinson without the approval of the Barkagarh *zamindars*. This disturbed the peaceful life of his ladies of the *harem*. Similarly, after some years German missionaries came to Ranchi and established church there. They founded a new religion. Thus the sanctity of the Jagarnnath Temple at Barkagarh was believed to be violated and the families of the *zamindar* were virtually encircled by outsiders.[35]

On the other hand, Pandey Ganpat Rai also wanted to regain some political power in this new situation. He thought that during mutiny as a commander-in-chief of the rebels he would help the Emperor of Delhi with this Battalion of Chotanagpur to defeat the British. He expected that in return he would be awarded with some *sanad* from the Emperor who would enhance his power and prestige in Chotanagpur.[36] Due to all these reasons Thakur Biswanath Shahdeo and Ganpat Rai agreed to cooperate with the mutineers. Biswanath Shahdeo became the chief and Ganpat Rai the commander-in-chief of the rebel sepoys.[37] But as against this the Maharaja of Chotanagpur and other *zamindars* not only supported the British but also helped suppress the movement.[38]

However, after occupying the Ranchi town, Biswanath Shahdeo used to hold his *darbar* at Doranda in a bangalow and administered justice. He directed some of his followers to cut the Ranchi Ramgarh Road and for this a Ghatwal of Ramgarh Luther Singh, helped Bishwanath Shahdeo. He disrupted Ranchi Ramgarh Road by cutting trenches so that the British force might not reach Ranchi.[39] The rebels decided to go to Sherghati *via* Chatra to meet Babu Kunwar Singh of Jagdishpur there. They started for Sherghati on 11 September, 1857. Before leaving Ranchi, they looted the town and insulted some ladies also. All the bungalows of British officers were burnt down and the Police Lines destroyed.[40]

The mutineers reached Ramgarh Ghat on 14 September but they found that the *zamindars* of Chouriya, Bhola Singh was ready to check the rebels. He wanted to stop the mutineers there till the arrival of the British force. The mutineers fought with Bhola Singh but they could not get success. However, they proceeded to Balumath on 21 September and from there they reached Chatra on 30 September. Reaching Chatra they first indulged themselves in looting the town.[41] As Dalton was busy, Major English was directed to proceed to Ranchi. He reached Ranchi on 22 September with a force. He controlled the administration of the town. Col. Dalton reached Ranchi on 23 September and took control of the town. The court in the town started functioning. Missionaries also returned and normalcy was restored.[42]

Major English proceeded to Chatra to quell the rebellion. At Chatra, the rebels were defeated by the surprise attack of the British army which consisted of the army led by Major Simpson, Lt. J.C.C. Dontt, Sergent Dictom etc. Madhav Singh and his sepoys fled away from the battle field. Most of the rebels proceeded to Sherghati and dispersed. This battle was a decisive one. There were heavy losses to both sides. Lack of intelligence about the British Movement, loss of sympathy of the local people on account of plunder committed by the mutineers, desertion of Madhav Singh and the strong arms and ammunition of the British especially Enfield Rifles were some of the main causes of the defeat of the mutineers.[43] Lastly, Jaimangal Pandey and Nadir Ali, the rebel leaders, were captured on 3 October and were hanged on a tree next day. Biswanath Shahdeo and Ganpat Rai fled away to Lohardaga.[44]

Though many sepoys of Biswanath Shahdeo were captured and hanged near Ranchi Court, Thakur Biswanath Shahdeo and Ganpat Rai were out of bounds. Dalton himself reached Lohardaga and with the help of Biswanath Dubey and Mahesh Narayan Sahi, Major Nation arrested Biswanath Sahdeo and Ganpat Rai in March 1858. Both of them were hanged near the old Commissioner Compound on a tree on Friday, 16th April and 21st April, 1858 respectively.[45] During the time of hanging when Bishwanath Shahdeo hesitated to go to the altar of hanging, Ganpat Rai encouraged him and bravely said—*'Charhu Thakur Mati Daru Fansi, Kailanhi Person to Hobon Rour Sathi'*. (Climb Thakur, don't be afraid. Day after tomorrow, I will be also your friend.)[46] With this encouragement Thakur Bishwanath Shahdeo dedicated his life to the country. After the death of all the rebel leaders, the mutiny came to an end. Thus all the freedom fighters dedicated their life on the altar of freedom.

During the Rebellion of 1857-58 the *zamindars* taking advantage of the absence of the authorities oppressed and plundered the native converts.[47] Some of the *zamindars* had usurped the land and property of the indigenous people.[48] But after the mutinee on the restoration of law and order the refugee aboriginals received assistance from the relief fund to enable them to cultivate their land.[49] This support encouraged the tribals and it aroused craving for freedom.[50] As the native converts were compensated against their losses, an impression gained ground among them that they were a favourable people of the government. This added strength to these people. As a result, they claimed all their ancestral lands back which had been taken by the *thikadars*.[51] Thus the Rajhas land[52] of the indigenous people which the *thikadars* and *zamindars* had captured before was again asserted as Bhuinhari land[53] and recaptured. These indigenous people broke the law and disturbed the area. Thus there started an affray in some of the areas in Chotanagpur.[54]

The first conflict between the native Christians and their landlords started in 1858 at Basia and Sonpur Pargana. In the month of October 1858, *zamindars* Babu Shib Narain Sahi proceeded to the village of Jhapra to collect rent. But the Christians who lived in the adjacent area resisted and there started an affray against the *zamindars*. They captured his horses and two men and the *zamindars* was driven out from the village.[55] In November 1858, again a conflict started in the village Bala. Anand Singh, Jagirdar of Bala, Thakur Jadunath Sahi and his force who attempted to collect rent by force were resisted by the *bhuihars* or original settlers of the village. These indigenous people opposed force with force. The result was that an affray ensued therein which two men of *jagirdar* were killed. Three men, one servant of Thakur, and a horse and some arms were captured and taken by the Christians to the sub-Assistant Commissioner at Ranchi, together with the body of one of the men slain in the affray and there lodged their complaints.[56] This is not the end: a serious incident again took place in 1859 at a village called Ghagari. In this case a land disputes started between a Christian Munda named Bari and one Karam Singh, a Jagirdar. A free fight ensued between them in which the Jagirdar and two of his followers were killed and Bari was wounded and soon afterwards died in Jail.[57] Thus disorder prevailed more or less throughout the Pargana Bussia, Bellcuddee and Doesa.

Taking advantage of this confusion, the indigenes forcibly recaptured their old *Bhuinhari* land. However Government dispatched a detachment to assist the local police in preserving law and order in Pargana Sonepur and Bussia. Thus the disputes did not again break out to the same alarming extent.[58] In this way, these native converts asserted their right over the *rajhas* land. But after the suppression of the disturbances by Government, *zamindars* started to exploit these indigenous people. The Government seriously discussed the question of registering the special tenures of Chotanagpur. The authorities thought that the only effective mode of preventing repetition of these affrays and riots would be to ameliorate the grievances that had given rise to them. Thus according to the Government order on 15 April, 1858, Lal Lokenath Sahi, a local *zamindars* and Sub-Assistant Commissioner were deputed to prepare a register of all *Bhuinhari* lands. This Officer began his operation in August 1860. During this period, his enquiries extended to 572 villages, out of which he could complete the registers of 429 villages only while those of 143 villages were left incomplete. The Parganas in which he carried on his investigations were Lodhma, Khukra, Udaipur, Sonepur, Doesa, Korambe, and Bussia.[59]

However, due to this survey for the time being, it pacified the Mundas and Oraons remained quiet as they thought that their rights would be protected. But with this the death of Lal Lokenath Sahi on 13 August, 1862, the survey stopped and again disputes between landlords and tenants broke out.[60] The result was that these indigenous people again started a movement for reoccupying their *Bhuinhari* land. This movement is known as *Sardari Larai* or *Mulkui Larai* against the *jagirdars* which ultimately became the base of Birsa Movement in Jharkhand.[61]

## NOTES & REFERENCES

1. B. Virottam, Jharkhand, *Itihas Avam Sanskriti*, Ranchi, 2004, p. 79.
2. "When the oppressor wants a horse, the Kol must pay: When he desires a Palki, the Kols have to pay, and afterwards to bear him therein. They must pay for his musicians, for his milch cows, for his *Pan*. Does some one die in his house? He taxes them; is a child born? again a tax; is there a marriage or *puja*? a tax; Is the *thikadar* found guilty at *cutchary* and sentenced to be punished? The Kol must pay the fine or does a death occur in the house of the Kol? The poor man must pay a fine. Is a child born? Is a son or daughter married? The poor Kol is still taxed. And this plundering, punishing, robbing system goes on till the Kols run away". S.C. Roy, *Mundas and their Country*, Calcutta, 1912, p. 221, Virottam, *Jharkhand*, p. 214.
3. Virottam, *Jharkhand*, p. 407-08.
4. *Ibid.*, pp. 215-16.
5. *Ibid.*, p. 214.
6. Roy, *The Mundas*, pp. 201-211, L.S.S. O'Malley, Singhbhum, Saraikela and Kharsawan, Calcutta, 1910, p. 35.
7. J.C. Jha, *The Tribal Revolt of Chotanagpur*, (1831-32) Patna, 1987, pp. 164-172.
8. Romila Thapar and Majid Hayat Siddigi, *Chotanagpur : The Pre-Colonial and Colonial Situation*, in R.D. Munda and S. Bosu Mullick (ed): *The Jharkhand Movement, Copenhagen*, 2003, p. 48.
9. J. Reid, *Final Report on the Survey and Settlement operation in the District of Ranchi, 1907-1910*, Calcutta, 1912, p. 34; J.C. Jha, *The Tribal Revolts*, p. 41.
10. K. Shital, *Chotanagpur Ki Kalisia Ka Britant*, Allahabad, 1940, pp. 4-9, S.P. Sinha, *Conflict and Tension in Tribal Society*, New Delhi, 1993, pp. 96, 97.
11. Sinha, Conflict, pp. 98-101.
12. Roy, *The Mundas*, p. 228; Sinha, *Conflict*, pp. 106-107.
13. Roy, *The Mundas*, p. 230.
14. Panjika, 2005 (A Hindi Annual Magazine of G.E.L. Church, Ranchi.) p. 31.
15. S.P. Sinha, *Life and Times of Birsa Bhagwan*, Ranchi, 1963, p. 39., S.P. Sinha, *Conflict*, p. 101.
16. Roy, *The Mundas*, p. 199.
17. Virottam, *Jharkhand*, p. 274.
18. *Ibid.*, p. 275.
19. S.P. Sinha, *Life and Times*, p. 39., S.P. Sinha, Conflict, p. 101.
20. Captain, J.S. Davies to the Commissioner of Chotanagpur, dated, 15 March, 1859, No. 156, Paper relating to Chotanagpur Agrarian

Disputes., p. 3., Roy, *The Mundas*, p. 226., P. Kumar, *Mutiny and Rebellion in Chotanagpur*, Patna, 1919, p. 99.

21. Roy, *The Mundas*, pp. 244-245.
22. P.C. Roy Choudhary, *Bihar Men 1857*, Patna, 1959, p. 112.
23. Roy, *The Mundas*, p. 230., Sinha, *Conflict*, p. 103.
24. Roy Choudhary, *Bihar Men*, pp. 45, 112., Virottam, *Jharkhand*, pp. 281-284., Kumar, Mutiny And, pp. 120-122.
25. Kumar, *Mutiny and Rebellion*, pp. 131-132., Virottam, *Jharkhand*, p. 284.
26. Virottam, *Jharkhand*, pp. 184-185.
27. Roy Chaudhary, *Bihar Men*, p. 112.
28. Kumar, *Mutiny and*, pp. 132-133.
29. Roy Chaudhary, *Bihar Men*, pp. 113-114.
30. During this mutiny all the Europeans fled to Calcutta and the missionaries had to leave their stations. The rebels attacked the church and plundered the benches and chairs and organ etc. The Christians were persecuted and ill treated. The Christian houses and villages were plundered and the inhabitants had to flee and at least spend six weeks in the jungles, mountains and caves without any other food than roots and leaves. Many of the fugitives died or got ill. The place where they took shelter is still known as Khristan Dera. S.C. Roy, *The Mundas*, pp. 230-31., *Ghar Bhandhu* a (Monthly Magazine of GEL Church Ranchi), March 2006, p. 24., July, 2007, pp. 19-22.
31. Chaudhary, *Bihar Men*, pp. 113-114.
32. Kumar, *Mutiny and Rebellion*, p. 156.
33. *Ibid.*, p. 155.
34. Virottam, *Jharkhand*, p. 288.
35. Kumar, *Mutiny and Rebellion*, pp. 98-106.
36. *Ibid.*, pp. 186-187.
37. Mathew Areeparampil, *Struggle for Swaraj*, Chaibasa, 2002, p. 165, Kumar, *Muntiy and Rebellion*, pp. 156, 187.
38. Roy Chaudhary, *Bihar Men*, pp. 111-112, Virottam, *Jharkhand*, p. 288.
39. Virottam, *Jharkhand*, p. 289.
40. *Ibid.*, p. 284.
41. *Ibid.*, pp. 292-293.
42. Roy Chaudhary, *Bihar Men*, p. 114.
43. Virottam, *Jharkhand*, pp. 294-295.
44. *Ibid*, p. 295.
45. Virottam, *Jharkhand*, pp. 295-297, Roy Chaudhary, Bihar Men, p. 114.
46. K. Shital, *Chotanagpur ki Kalisia ka Britant*, Allahabad, 1914, p. 145.
47. Captain J.S. Davies to the Commissioner, 15 March, 1859, Agrarian Papers, pp. 2-3.

48. Roy, *The Mundas*, pp. 239-240.
49. Sinha, *Life and Times*, p. 38.
50. Shital, *Chotanagpur Ki*, p. 45.
51. Petor Tete, a *Missionary Social Worker in India;* Fr. J. B. Hoffmann, Ranchi, 1986, p. 13.
52. *Land of the Jagirdars or Raja's Share in Munda Villages.*
53. The Bhuinhari Land is the ancestral property of the original settlers of Chotanagpur; it is a local variant of the Mundari Khunkatti.
54. John MacDaugall, *Land or Religion*, New Delhi, 1985, p. 40.
55. Roy, *The Mundas*, p. 241.
56. *Ibid.*, p. 242.
57. *Ibid.*, p. 245.
58. Resolution—By the Govt. of Bengal, Revenue Department dated Calcutta, the 25 November 1880, Paper relating to Agrarian Disputes, p. 88
59. Roy, *The Mundas*, pp. 269-270., MacDougall, *Land or Region*, p. 40
60. Roy, *The Mundas*, p. 270.
61. Suresh Singh, *The Dust Storm and Hanging Mist*, Calcutta, 1966, p. 26.

# 6

# *Mulkui Larai* in Chotanagpur
## *The Genesis and Impact*

A.K. CHATTORAJ

The post-mutiny period witnessed the *Sardars* agitation or *Mulkui Larai* (the struggle for land) in Chotanagpur. *Sardar* meant 'the leader' and the name was applied to the organizers of the movement but later those who took part in the movement were also called by the same name. It is essential to mention, right at the outset, some of the crucial sources[1] of information about the *Sardar* agitation. John MacDougall has dealt in detail with the *Sardar* Movement. Fidelis de Sa provides an in-depth study of the main grievances of the *Sardars* and the part played by missionaries in the movement. S.P. Sinha has, in course of discussing the background of the Birsa Movement, focuses on its connections with the *Sardar* agitation. K.S. Singh's *Birsa Munda* (National Book Trust, New Delhi) throws light on the different aspects of the *Sardar* agitation as a predecessor of the Birsa Movement. The Settlement Reports of 1910 (Reid) and missionary records of that period are also helpful. Rakhal Das Haldar's 'Final Report on the Settlement of Bhuinhari Tenures' in Bengal (1890) is also an important source of information.

Though the movement started earlier but it gained momentum after the failure of the Chotanagpur Tenures Act (1869)[2] and of the operations following on it—the Bhuinhari Survey and Settlement Operations. The agitation continued for four decades and constituted the background of the Birsa Movement.

The tribal area of Chotanagpur was seething with agrarian discontent owing to the ignorance of the British about the socio-economic systems of the aboriginals. This resulted in a number of rebellions, prominent among them being the *Kol* rebellion of 1831-32 and the *Santal* rebellion of 1855-56. Neither the creation of the South West Frontier Agency in 1834[3] nor the creation of commissionership of the Chotanagpur Division two decades later addressed the basic issues affecting the tribes of Chotanagpur. The *Hos, Cheros* and *Bhogtas* participated in the Revolt of 1857. In fact, some of the modern research scholars are of the view that the rebellion of 1857 occurred in Singhbhum because of the pre-existing agrarian grievances[4] following the conquest of Singhbhum and the formation of the Kolhan Government State in 1837, agrarian grievances had intensified as a result of the British intrusion into this region. The *Mundas* and *Oraons* by and large did not participate in the revolt of 1857.

After the conflicts and affrays that had occurred in the *Paraganas* of Sonepur and Basia in the year 1858 were suppressed, the *Munda* country was again restless. The government seriously discussed the question of registering land tenures of Chotanagpur in order to prevent repetition of such riots.[5] Lal Lokenath Shahi, a local *zamindar,* was appointed under the Government orders dated 15 April, 1858 to prepare a register of all *bhuinhari* lands. Till his death in 1862, Shahi completed his enquiries in respect of 427 villages. After his death nothing was done to complete his work. Shahi's decisions were on the whole more favourable to landlords than to *bhuinhars;* naturally *Mundas* were not satisfied.[6]

The spread of Christianity around the second half of the nineteenth century gave a new turn to the agrarian question. The motive of the *Mundas* in joining the German Mission was not purely spiritual. They hoped that the German missionaries would check the malpractices of the *zamindars*[7]. From 1850 to 1859 the *zamindars* reacted sharply against the missionaries coming to the help of Christian *ryots*[8]. The landlords found that the converted Christian *ryots* no longer willingly submitted to their illegal demands, therefore, soon after the conversions began in 1850, the landlords began a stronger form of oppression against the converts than before. During the mutiny, the *zamindars,* taking advantage of the absence of authorities, oppressed and plundered the native converts, many of whom were forced to flee to jungles. On the restoration of law and order, refugee aboriginals received assistance from the relief fund of the Government to enable them to cultivate their land, leading to a level of independence that irritated the landlords.[9]

Forty years of the *Sardars'* agaitation of *Mulkui Larai* from 1858 onwards constituted the background of Birsa Movement. Like the leaders of previous insurrections the *Sardars* claimed to be the original settlers. Aiming to expel the *zamindars,* they protested against the incidence of forced labour. They adopted means of 'prayer, petition and protest' to win back their freedom. They collected funds to fight legal battles for the restoration of their lost rights and land, stimulated by the memory of the golden past of the tribes free from *dikus,* and at one stage urged to be taken under direct British administrations. They were not disloyal to the Crown, not even to the Raja of Chotanagpur in the initial stages. Occasionally they turned out the rent collectors and did not pay rent, and sought forcible occupation of their ancestral lands, which the landlords had captured[10]. The Bhuinhari Survey and Settlement under Chotanagpur Tenures Act (Act II of 1869)[11] aimed at making for each village an accurate register of all the tenants. Special commissioners were authorized to restore to possession all persons who had been wrongfully dispossessed during the past two decades and to enter their names in the village register as occupants of the land. The Act made special provisions to enable everyone to file a suit before the special commissioners for the recovery of their lands. The Government thus admitted that the aboriginals had been wronged by the aliens and efforts would be made to restore to them what they had lost. The Act, however, did not define *bhuinhari* land. Foreign landlords were opposed by the aboriginals when they tried to capture *bhuinhari patties.*

Investigations of the *Bhuinhari* lands began on 1 April, 1869 and continued till 31 March, 1880. As many as 13,473 claims[12] were disposed[13]. The operations could not protect people against future attacks on their ancestral land nor could it restore the land to those who had been wrongfully dispossessed during the past two decades. They excluded the *Manki patties*[14] which were the heart of the *Munda* country (present south-western Ranchi district) and which preserved the ancient land system of the *Mundas*. The settlement caused the *Mundas* and the *Oraons* to lose more of their lands and increased unrest in the area. Antagonism between the landlords and tenants continued to be as strong as ever. The aboriginals then began collecting money and prepared petitions to the Government in defence of their rights. These petitions, however, were turned down[15] As the *Mundas* continued sending petitions, the officials regarded this as agitation, and later this form of appeal was called the *Sardars* Agitation.

Early in 1867, the aboriginals sent a petition to the Commissioner of Chotanagpur, complaining against oppression by the landlords. It included complaints like ejection of tenants from the land by taking away the land and repeated collection of rent without giving any receipt. The commissioner rejected the petition. An appeal to the Lieutenant Governor dated 21 September, 1867 met the same fate. These petitions must have a bearing upon the passing of the Chotanagpur Tenures Act of 1869 and the Survey and Settlement that went with it.[16] There is no doubt that the movement gained momentum after the failure of the act.

The missionaries took up the cases of the aboriginals and wrote to the Lieutenant Governor about the grievances of the people, which also fell on deaf ears. The people continued to send petitions, as *Sardars* were not satisfied with the settlement operation and were not ready to accept anything short of a restoration of all the lands that they or their ancestors had ever possessed.

The petition to the Commissioner of Chotanagpur in March 1879 contained the signature of 14,000 Christians, in which the complaint was made that the measurement of the *bhuinhari* lands was not done properly. The claims of the *Mundas* were ignored. The *Mundas* claimed that Chotanagpur belonged to them since the area had been possessed by their ancestors. The commissioner rejected the petition and then the memorialists appealed to the Secretary of State for India, London. They added some more points, like they are allowed to form into village communities directly under the Government. Lord Hartington, the Secretary of State for India, rejected the petition. He held that the Bhuinhari Survey was the utmost the Government could do for them and steps were to be taken to put a stop to further agitation. The Commissioner addressed to the missionaries to implement the orders from London and the latter readily promised to desist Christians from collecting subscription and getting up petitions to reverse decisions on which the final orders of the highest authorities had pronounced.[17] But assistance to the Government antagonized the aborigines against the Lutheran Mission. The animosity of the *Sardars* reached its height in 1887. Dr Nottrott, one of the Lutheran missionaries, seeing the *Sardars* using force, took the matter to court.

Several of those who left the Lutheran Mission joined the Catholic Mission,[18] which by that time had gained popularity under Fr. Lievens. Lievens sent catechists who spoke to villagers on market days about the assistance given by the missionaries in court cases. He advised the people to pay the legal amount of rent and landlord services as approved by custom and to insist on a receipt. If the landlords ill-treated the people they should be taken to court. He explained law to them and pointed out their legal obligations before British Law.[19] He would even give loans to people if necessary. Like the Lutherans he regarded the *Sardar* movement an agitation; probably he tried to be in the good books of the Government officials by supporting the Government position. As a result of his efforts a large number of *Oraons* who were formerly Lutherans were converted to Catholicism, on the condition that they were to give up their efforts for *Raj*. They were to pay landlords the rent and services that were due according to law and custom, neither more nor less. During 1889-90, the number of Catholics swelled, and the Government warned the missionaries not to meddle with land questions. About 200 Roman catechists were arrested and then let off. Lievens also left Torpa and the influences of Roman Catholic Mission waned on the *Sardars*.[20]

In 1880 Power, the Deputy Commissioner of Lohardaga, expressed concern over the relations between landlords and tenants in his district. He studied the history of aboriginals and came to recognize their traditional socio-economic organizations. He asserted that the *jagirdars* had only the right to rent, but they had taken over the land. The Chotanagpur Tenures Act of 1869 did not prove a panacea for these troubles.

Meanwhile the *Sardars* continues to send memorials. In 1882 Power reported that a fresh petition was sent to London in which, among other things, the demand was made for permission to be given to the village communities of Chotanagpur to come to direct settlement with the Government without the intervention of the *thickadars*; and opportunities be offered to the petitioners to reclaim the jungles and to hold the reclaimed lands as village communes under the settlement with the Government. However, the Secretary of State turned down the petition in 1882. Similar memorials were sent in 1884. These too seem to have been rejected.

In 1886-87, the agitation broke out again. The Government stand was that the *bhuinhari* settlement of 1869 was the utmost the Government could do. The repetition of the same demands made no sense to them; hence, the petitions were rejected. The *Mundas* and the *Oraons* continued to be discontented; they felt let down by the Government.[21] The memorialists believed that decrees had been obtained which recognized their claims. Stevens, the Commissioner, tried to convince the leaders that they were being duped by their advisors, the lawyers of Calcutta; and in fact no decree had been obtained. Still, the agitators considered themselves as the lords of the soil and refused to pay rent. The memorial of 1887 met the same fate as all others.

By 1890, the honeymoon of the agitators with the missions was over. They had realized that the Roman Catholic Mission could rid them of *zamindars* no more than the Lutheran Mission. They accused all the missionaries of being hand in glove with local officials and maintained that all Europeans had turned hostile to the aborigines and decided to fight alone for their land.[22] To approach the Viceroy and the Queen the *Sardars* started collection from the villages and left for Calcutta in order to engage lawyers, who showed them several false documents of *Munda* Raj and were told that the Queen had granted their requests but the decree had been hidden from them by missionaries.

The constitutional methods had not yielded the desired results. So some of the *sardars* understood the futility of carrying on the agitations but a few of their isolated groups still engaged Jacob, an English barrister, to plead their cases. A new group of people, *neo-sardars,* who thought that the root of their plight was the British government, which protected their enemies and must be overthrown, emerged. In September 1892, these *sardars* hatched a plot to kill all *thickadars* and German missionaries, but failed, as they had no organization.

The agitation had passed through, according to Dr. K.S. Singh, a revivalist phase during the eighth decade of the nineteenth century. In 1881, a party of *sardars* calling themselves the "Children of Mael" under one John the Baptist set up a kingdom at Doesa and proclaimed a *Raj* of their own. S.C. Roy views this incident as a ludicrously comic show at Doesa by a small band of malcontents styling themselves as "Children of Mael" who established themselves on the ruins of the *Garh* of Doesa.[23]

Frustrated with the missionaries and disappointed by the Government attitude, they looked forward to the advent of a leader, and thus Birsa found at the time of his rise a situation that suited him best. Some people regard Birsa as a stooge of the *sardars* and view his movement as a continuation of the *Sardari Larai*, but the basic difference between these movements was that while the former was not anti-government, Birsa refused to acknowledge any authority superior to him. The *Sardari Larai* was not disloyal; Birsa placed himself at the head of *Munda* Raj and threw off the allegiance altogether. The two movements had similar cause at the origin, long years of brooding and discontent among the *Mundas* and in the end both merged there is controversy as to whether Birsa was inspired by the teachings of the *sardars,* or the *sardars* joined him as that suited them the most. The *sardars,* finding their own agitation fruitless, offered as a last resort to fall with Birsa's plans. Birsa certainly was influenced by *Sardars,* but the latter lacked positive programmes. Birsa had a distinctively different line of action. The *Sardars* opposed violent revolt as a deliberate tactic, and never demanded the end of British rule in India. Between 1858-1895 they never gave up submitting petitions to the highest levels of British Government—which implies that the *sardars* accepted the legitimacy of the supreme British authorities.[24]

## NOTES & REFERENCES

1. John MacDougall, *Land or Religion?,* Manohar Publication, New Delhi, 1985; Fidelis de Sa, *Crisis in Chotanagpur* Redemptionist Publication, Bangalore, 1975; S.P. Sinha, *Life and Times of Birsa Bhagwan,* Bihar Tribal Research Institute, Ranchi, 1964.
2. Act provided for an extensive land investigation and a thorough demarcation of *bhuinhari* tenures and landlords' privileged lands. The *bhuinhari* survey lasted from 1869 to 1880 and covered 27% of the district villages.
3. The South West Frontier Agency was created in 1834 with its headquarters at Kishanpur (Ranchi). Captain Wilkinson was the first Governor-General's Agent of the Agency.
4. S. Das Gupta, 'Rebellion in a Little Known District of the Empire', in Sabyasachi Bhattacharya (ed.) *Rethinking 1857.* Orient Longman, New Delhi, 2007, p. 113.
5. Fidelis de Sa, *Crisis in Chotanagpur,* Redemptionist Publication, Bangalore, 1975, p. 60.
6. Shahi began his operations in August 1860. During two years of his works he could complete the registers of 429 villages. *Mundas* accused Shahi of being biased in favour of landlords. But some *bhuinhari* rights were given legal protection and much *bhuinhari* land was restored that had been alienated during the Revolt of 1857. S.C. Roy, *Mundas* and their country, Crown Publications, Ranchi, 2004, p. 146.

7. German Lutherans were the first missionaries to work in Ranchi district. They arrived in 1845 but the mission grew steadily only after the Revolt of 1857. In 1869 the mission split into two. The Society for the Propagation of the Gospel, an Anglican Mission, had modest growth in late nineteenth century. Fidelis de Sa, *Crisis*, p. 184.
8. K.S. Singh, *Birsa Munda*, p. 7.
9. S.P. Sinha, *Life and Times of Birsa Bhagwan*, Bihar Tribal Research Institute, Ranchi, 1964, p. 37.
10. Singh, *Birsa Munda*, p. 8.
11. The Chotanagpur Tenures Act (Act II of 1869) was passed in 1869 with a view to an authoritative settlement of the title to *bhuinhari* lands. The arrangements made by this act are also called the Bhuinhari Survey and Settlement. By this act the Lieutenant Governor was empowered to appoint special commissioners to investigate claims to tenures and demarcate lands. They were to make, for each village, an accurate register of all the tenants. They were also empowered to restore to possession all persons who had been wrongfully dispossessed during the 20 years preceding the act. The act, however, could not protect the people against future attacks on their ancestral lands; nor was it successful in its stated endeavour.
12. The operations extended to 2,482 villages in 35 *Paraganas* of the Lohardaga (Ranchi) district. Fidelis de Sa, *Crisis*, pp. 60-61.
13. *Ibid.*, p. 63.
14. Some of the Mundas had emigrated to other parts of Chotanagpur to escape the rule of the *Raja*, and started new villages. They organized these villages into *Manki patties*. The *Raja* collected contributions from the *Mankis*. Those Mundas who did not emigrate formed *bhuinhar patties* where the *Raja* later began collecting the contributions and tribute directly from each village. *Ibid.*, p. 62.
15. In a petition submitted by Jugdeep Joseph, Manamasse Chumna Co, and around 14,000 Christians dated 25 March, 1879, the petitioners complained to the Commissioner of Chotanagpur that the measurement of the *bhuinhari* lands was not properly done and the same was done as dictated by the *thickadars*, ignoring the claims to their ancestral lands and consequently, the oppression by the *thickadars* continued. Roy, *The Mundas*, p. 153. The German Mission submitted a petition dated 17 May, 1876, complaining against the native Commissioner and calling for the abolition of manifold imposts and taxes, etc. K.S. Singh, *Birsa Munda*, p. 9.
16. Fidelis de Sa, *Crisis*, p. 112.

17. The Government officials regarded the collecting of money and sending memorials as political agitation after 1869. Since many of the *Sardars* were believed to be Christians, the Government grew suspicious of the mission and the missionaries. *Ibid*, pp. 176-177.
18. The first Jesuit missionary in the region, Stockman, arrived in Chotanagpur on 24 November, 1868 and established the first Catholic mission station at Chaibasa. Their progress, to begin with, was very slow. The first Catholic chapel was built in 1874 at Burundi near Khunti. By 1885, the number of baptized *Mundas* of this mission counted to 2,092; Roy, *The Mundas*, pp. 158-159.
19. The early Jesuit Fathers, up to 1885, restricted themselves to missionary work. They did not favour helping the people with their court cases. Yet, mere preaching and mercy were not what the people wanted. Lievens decided to help the people within the law, to get assistance from the law against the injustices of the landlords. He also decided to keep the favour of the British officials, who at times looked with suspicion at the means used by the Father. Before 1889, he had occasion to answer the Commissioner for certain false accusations made against the Jesuits. Fidelis de Sa, *Crisis*, pp. 161-162.
20. Singh, *Birsa Munda*, p. 10.
21. Fidelis de Sa, *Crisis*, p. 181.
22. Sinha, *Life and Times of Birsa Bhagwan*, p. 41.
23. Roy, *The Mundas*, p. 154.
24. MacDougall, *Land or Religion?*, p. 62.

# 7

# Alien Construct and Tribal Contestation in Colonial Chotanagpur

## *The Medium of Christianity*

JOSEPH BARA

*The Compact Edition of the Oxford English Dictionary* (1971) explains the original meaning of 'tribe' as 'a group of persons forming a community and claiming descent from a common ancestor'. The etymology changed it in course of time as 'a race of people . . . applied especially to a primary aggregate of people in a primitive or barbarous condition under a headman or chief'. The change from the tribe being a kinship-based simple community to its being a group in 'primitive and barbarous condition' marks a distinct derogation of the term. Paradoxically, this took place in modern times—an age of liberal and revolutionary ideas on man and society—and the derogatory concept was indiscriminately used to stamp certain groups as incorrigible backwards in various parts of the colonial world. Especially in the early twentieth century, the Darwinist theory of race was brought into use to depict tribes as less human and more beastly, somewhat in a following way: 'There is less difference between the highest type of ape and lowest of aborigines than there is between the latter and the modern English gentleman'.[1] Today, a tribe is universally understood as primitive, savage or wild in a routine manner.

This conceptual vilification was entirely based on non-tribal sources. Rarely were the tribal view points taken into account, since those who indulged in it belonged to the exploiting classes. Colonially evolved concept was, thus, imposed on the tribals. The imposition meant suppression of the tribals' own idea of tribalness which insisted on a tribe being simply a human, no less or no more, though a tribal might be living a simple and contented life.[2] Based on this conviction, recently an Indian tribal group voiced its concern: '. . . little respect is today, shown to our culture, social systems, political structures and economy. Efforts are made to integrate us into the mainstream society as a low caste, though traditionally we have lived in an egalitarian and casteless society'.[3] This essay attempts to examine, taking the case of the Mundas and Uraons of Chotanagpur, how the term 'tribe' was shaped and how tribes of India responded to the conceptual cultural imposition under British colonialism.

**Resilient Tribal Identity**

Under the British colonial rule, most of the tribal populations have a history of resistance of the outsiders for their nefarious acts of encroachment and exploitation.[4] Even after Independence, many, with a strong sense of sons-of-the soil, have continued to assert for their rights. This tempts one to project tribes as avowed subaltern fighters for property rights, but nonchalant on their cultural identity. A careful observation indicates that the tribal societies are actually highly aware of their self-defined cultural identity. A live indigenous tribal identity is an integral part of any tribal awakening for rights, whether a revolt or a movement, though its expression might be latent in some cases. The tribals' tribal identity, often reiterated and redefined, differed distinctly from what was imposed. There are instances where the Mundas and Uraons based the claims of rights on their self-defined identity. Perhaps one of the best examples in this respect is their maiden demand for autonomy under the Indian polity, as a remedy to internal colonialism in their region, before the Indian Statutory Commission (1928). In their petition the tribals professed :

> We aborigines, sir . . . as descendants of the earliest known owners of Indian soil and with more hoary

> traditions of sovereignty in the land, . . . are entitled to as much or perhaps greater indulgence and an equal, if not a larger, share in the Government of our own people . . . These alien landlords despise us as *'Mlechhas'* and despicable creatures—more brutes than men, and actually stigmatize us as 'Kols' which we understand is a Sanskrit term for 'pigs'. But we too, sirs, are human beings with a long past—longer than that of any other race in India, with a native genius for democratic Government.[5]

Voices like this did not surface from, what is generally presumed, a cultural vacuum, or 'silence' of the suppressed subalterns.[6] They emanated rather from certain vibrant cultural undercurrent of the tribal society that found articulation under certain specific situation. The Western forces coming under the bogey of colonialism provided stimulus to the expression. But they were, it should be emphasized, not the source of it, as authors tend to argue fallaciously.[7] In 1831-32, for instance, when Western forces had hardly reached Chotanagpur, the tribals, being harassed and labelled as 'Kols' by their adversaries, spontaneously felt 'being of one caste [meaning tribe] and brethren' to rise against the enemies.[8]

Against live and resilient self-defined cultural identity, from mid-1830s the Mundas and Uraons closely encountered the forces of colonial education, British idea of rule by law and Christianity. These were introduced to pacify or tame the tribals, whom the colonial ethnography of the time portrayed as 'belligerent' or 'beastly', having animal-like loose emotions and low intellect. The interplay of these developments created a queer situation : more the cultural abuse of the tribals more was their cultural consciousness. If cultural impositions were innovative and sublime, the tribal responses were no less dynamic and reconstructive. In the whole situation, the role of missionized Christianity was central. Christianity, instead of subduing the tribal psyche, stimulated it to be more right-cum-identity-conscious, making the tribals employ Biblical analogies to define a respectable concept of tribe. This has been shown in the chapter in the later part.

**Conceptual Condemnation by Deprivation**

The prelude to the Munda and Uraon mind being locked in such dialogue is marked with a continuous conceptual reduction of tribe by the colonial state, making the tribals increasingly contemptible. The deprivation and exploitation of the tribals actually went hand in hand with conceptual despicability of tribe. Thus, the innocent-looking and frequently used eighteenth century British term 'hillman' or 'dhangar' (deriving from 'danga' or hill) for tribe[9] came to be replaced by such brutish variants as 'semi-barbarous', 'demon' or 'kol'[10] by the early nineteenth century. In this shift, invariably essence was drawn from the popular *Purana* of the eighteenth century, the *Bhavisyata Purana*.[11] A statement of 1832 reflects the change clearly :

> The inhabitants, neighbours to Coles [generally spelt Kol] are a simple and in-offensive race, are chiefly Hindoos and talk the Ooriah language. They have the greatest dread of the Coles, whom they consider as demons, and no doubt, from their former frequent aggressions, in which they usually exercised every species of cruelty, the former has sufficient cause for doing so. Having no religion, the Coles, during their incursions never hesitated to enter the temples.[12]

After 1850, when the Mundas and Uraons mustered courage, after an interregnum, to assert for their tribal rights under the *Sardari Larai* (1858-1890), they were despised and demonized further as '*sar kols*' (dirty kols), 'impure and illiterate savages', 'stubborn kols', 'restless junglies' and so forth.[13] Many of these abusive terms found their way in the official proceedings as common usage. The irony was that the agitating tribals associated with this movement made advanced use of recently acquired skill of rudimentary literacy in petitions and depositions for radical claims.[14] Even words like 'chuar' and 'dakait' (thief and dacoit respectively), hitherto used for certain neighbouring tribes, were freely imported and applied on the Mundas and Uraons.[15]

The beastly and demon connotation of the term normally attributed to Darwinian racism in anthropological literature, actually pre-existed in India for centuries. The *Vedas, Puranas* and epical writings like *Ramayana* are replete with reference of tribe as *dasyu, daitya, nisada, rakshasa* and so on, all invariably linked with the Aryan concept of *mlechchh*.[16] The tribes in these literatures generally remain beastly and monstrous, though some, in exceptional cases, were seen to turn humane under direct godly influence or brahminical ambassadorial touch of 'civilization'.[17] The term 'Uraon' was, thus, said to have derived from recitation of 'O! Ram' by a grieving *banara* when Lord Rama left his forest abode of fourteen years.[18]

Even the great nineteenth century enlightenment of colonial Bengal failed to bring any qualitative difference in the conceptual understanding. In late 1860s, a peer group of intelligentsia conjectured the following Indian tribe: 'The Hindu books in poetical legends describe those aborigines as monkeys, so Megasthenes writes of Indians one-eyed, without noses, wrapped up in the ears (*hastikarnas*): even Marco Polo and Ptolemy believed that men with tails had a real existence....'[19] Under static mindset, the Mundas and Uraons were further described by the same forum as 'Dhangars and other low caste people in the jungles: still impure, as probably unconverted *mlechchhas*'.[20]

## The Informants' Paradise

When colonial ethnography embarked upon defining the tribe, it relied upon the same traditional Hindu sources, now 'orientalized' for the colonial purposes. The local Indian idea of tribe, thus, colluded with the racist idea, demeaning the concept greatly. Here an important role was played by the local informants of the Europeans coming from the plains, who, as internal colonizers of the tribal regions, were highly prejudiced against the tribal people. They were not only gate-keepers of information on the tribals, but were also active disinformants, out to prove that the tribals were by no means land-owners, but nondescript 'turbulent rebel'.[21] The early sixty years of the

British rule facilitated the informants' disinformation politically. The authorities governed the region from camp offices at Chatra and Sherghati in central Bihar, which meant to the tribals a distant 'Delhi durbar'.[22]

From around the mid-nineteenth century, some European administrator-ethnographers stationed themselves in the tribal regions and encountered the tribals directly. This accessed them to a new kind of information that projected a tribe different than what was colonially shaped and espoused. The tribals were found to possess certain noble human qualities—bravery, fidelity, honesty, diligence and intelligence—tempting the authorities as 'splendid material for recruiting regiments equal to best of our native army'.[23] But this did not lead to any conceptual rediscovery. In the face of escalating tribal resistance to the colonial rule, the colonial state was bent upon showing the tribes as barbarous backwards. This inspired the colonial ethnographical project to remain firm on its charter and comfortable with the existing approach and information syndicate. Moreover, the outsiders, now migrating into the region in larger numbers and having greater economic stake, came to monoplolize the expanded British bureaucracy at the crucial subordinate level. The period, thus, became the informants' paradise.

Unprecedented dominance of the alien informants in the colonial information regime sealed the tribal viewpoints from reaching the European authorities. The colonial ethnological exercise, thus, essentially recycled and ratified the traditional Indian idea of tribe. The informants always played a proxy for the European ethnographers. In case of the Mundas and Uraons an avid observer noted this in the early twentieth century :

> No literary method is more fondly resorted by old bards—and probably, no habit was more important among the Aryan invaders [whose descendants the informants were]—than the giving of nicknames to the aboriginal tribes across whose path they had thrown themselves ... [The nicknaming] did duty, to all intents and purposes, for the real name.[24]

By reinforcing the pre-colonial stigma and adding the ingredient of Western racism, the colonial ethnography demonized and maligned the Mundas and Uraons as never before.[25]

**The Tribes' Tribal Sensitivity**

As those who reclaimed land from dense forest and made the region habitable, the Mundas and Uraons had strong attachment to the land, forest and other resources of Chotanagpur. Having been constantly pushed from one place to another, they had chosen to live in the place a peaceful and contented life and with simple needs. Centuries of living a relatively isolated life amidst forest and mountains helped them to develop and standardize a local culture. When outsiders began trickling in, the tribals accommodated them in their settlement, but in a separate part of the village and sans certain privileges of traditional tribal rights.[26] This way they became proud descendants of the first *'bhuinhars'* or original settlers before the migrants.

Used to democratic values, where their chiefs were simply *primus inter pares*, the Mundas and Uraons did not reconcile to the economic and cultural injustice and the idea of ruler-and-the-ruled that came with the outsiders. In the beginning the tribal cultural were actually forced the Nagabansi Raja, a migrant ruler, who had usurped power from Manki (Munda chief), to recognize the tribal way of life and even adopt it for several centuries. Things changed from the medieval times, when the Raja began distancing himself from the community of the tribals and invited a horde of outsiders as subordinates. Brahmins especially became his advisors and confidants. The immigrants were sublet the tribal lands fraudulently and were accorded the facility of free labour by imposing *bethbegari* (forced labour) on the tribals.

Culturally the Raja changed his colour by Hinduizing himself, an example that inspired some tribals at the upper echelon to follow the suit. This, what is called 'Great Tradition' or emulation of the Hindu rank model, is explained to be the tribals' natural tendency to discard their cultural values.[27] Far from this, the tribals actually adopted Hindu cultural traits as a strategy to protect their tribal cultural identity.[28] Thus, not to be surprised at, the so-called 'Great Tradition' went on side by side the 'tribalization' of the migrants in some tribe-dominated regions.[29] One is also reminded here of the Mundas and Uraons claiming their ancestry to the *Mahabharata* figure, Jarasandha while arguing for their 'indigenous' tribal status in Chotanagpur before the Indian Statutory Commission, 1928.[30]

The alienation of the Raja from the rank and file tribals and the rise of the migrants' dominance in the medieval times set off the malady of conceptual diminution of the Mundas and Uraons. The Raja now projected the tribals as people of 'low caste, turbulent wretches, in person like men, but in mind like beasts.'[31] Thus, the annals of the Nagabansis traced the lineage of Phani Mukut Rai, the first Raja who was an ordinary migrant, to a respectable Brahminical ancestry, whereas that of Madra Manki (whom the Raja had dislodged) to a 'cook' of 'one Bairaja Dom'.[32] The tribal chiefs, who defied the Raja, were called *'Daitya'* or *'Raksal'*.[33] As the outsiders' dominance took the shape of 'feudalism giving rise to every species of extortion and plunder', the abuse was unabated.[34] Not surprisingly, in the Moghul establishment the tribals were known mainly as the 'original savage race' or the 'barbarous Hindus of Jharkhand'.[35] Moghuls, it should be noted, ruled Chotanagpur through the Nagabansi Raja and saw the tribal society through the lens of the Raja's advisors and coterie.

Cultural disfiguration and slandering at the hands of the migrants boiled the blood of the Mundas and Uraons. Though harassed a lot, the tribals did not spare the enemies uncontested. The aliens—initially simply 'others' to the tribals'—became their hated *dikus* or exploiting aliens. To express their hatred for them, the tribals used the choicest metaphors, such as 'greedy vulture', 'ravenous crow', 'upstart peacock', 'ominous owl' and so on.[36] From their cultural standards, the tribals even looked down upon them as people of 'low birth'.[37] The tribals always simmered with antipathy towards the adversaries and were culturally repulsive.

## Colonial Malady and 'God-send' Christianity

The conceptual sensitivity of the Mundas and Uraons rose steadily since colonialism propped up the pre-colonial process of the tribals' deprivation. The tribal mind was not numbed even in the phase of, what is believed to be, their 'complete silence' or 'sullen silence' stunned by stern actions of the powerful British military in the early nineteenth century.[38] The suppression of the great revolt of 1831-32 actually became an opportunity for it to ruminate over the efficacy of the mode of violence for their cultural rehabilitation.

At this time the British gestured to the tribals a policy of friendship and assured redress for injustice on them in the post-revolt administrative measures of 1834. The British polity, insisting on administration by rule of law and justice, came to the doorstep of the tribals with headquarters at Kishenpur (present Ranchi). The first European officials posted in the region, led by Political Agent to the Governor-General, T. Wilkinson who established personal rapport with the tribals, promised to be the protector of the tribals. The British overture of goodwill, coming against the tribals' long experience of systematic deprivation by deceit and treachery by all the incoming social groups was most appealing.

Yet, even as the tribals responded to the British overture and tried to understand the 'benevolent' administration, they also found the ground reality unchanged. The alien landlords and the subordinate officials continued with their usual excesses, at times in a more reactionary way. For instance, the tribals, who had fled their villages fearing British reprisal in the course of the 1831-32 revolt and returned later to claim their land, were resisted.[39] This way the hollowness of British 'benevolence' was gradually vindicated and the measures of 1834 proved to be a mirage to the tribals. Deprivation of the tribals actually became more rampant and thorough. The euphoria of close connection to the European officials also dissipated. The officials were too preoccupied with the nitty-gritty of administrative reclamation of the region.

This premised the emergence of Christian missionaries as alternative well-wishers of the Mundas and Uraons. The urge of making the tribals a peaceable colonial subject remained strong in the British colonialist mind. This pushed the colonial managers to invite the missionaries as 'colonial social workers' to educate and 'civilize' the tribals.[40] The Gossner Evangelical Lutheran missionaries of Berlin responded to the colonialists' clarion call and positioned themselves among the tribals from 1845. To pursue their object of winning converts, the missionaries adopted, since 1850, a humanitarian approach to the tribal agrarian problems. The missionaries demonstrated their sympathy by providing consultancy to the tribals in their legal battle with the landlords and many tribals actually won back their lost rights. Reciprocally, the tribals converted to Christianity, which they found as such a simple belief, in large numbers.[41]

**Arming by Appropriation**

The progress of Christianity did not mean any check on the deprivation and denunciation of the tribals. The tribal mind was though tantalized by a series of surveys, reports and other official transactions of the colonial state that often upheld the *bhuinhari* status of the tribals and their distinct cultural identity.[42] Against this, the working of the constitutional means in the restoration of tribal rights through missionary mediation proved a magic to the tribals. It infused in the tribals a new confidence. The event also instilled in the tribal mind a deep faith in the British constitutional means, which was why profuse use of petitions and protracted course of the *Sardari Larai.*[43] As a result, the tribals retorted the claim of superiority of the Nagabansi Raja by asserting that they were actually the owners of land of Chotanagpur and the Raja was originally their 'servant'.[44]

While the Mundas and Uraons were busy experimenting with the appropriated 'resource' of British constitutionalism and Western education in the *Sardari Larai*[45], their engagement with Christianity became impassioned and deeper. From the beginning, the missionary actions fixed in the simple tribal mind the idea that the white missionaries were the right route to reach the white masters towards resolution of their problems.[46] Further, the missionaries continuing to help them, even at the risk of their own life, convinced the tribals that they were indeed their friends in need. This paved way for an intimate interface between the tribal society and Christianity.

In seeing the role of Christianity in the tribal society, scholars generally obscure the picture of reception by the tribals.[47] They leave no scope of the tribal mind being active and the possibility of reception being considered.[48] The whole approach is marked with the impatience of evaluating a vertical 'impact' of the 'alien' force of Christianity, bringing in instantly the cloud of Pax Christi or Pax Brittannica in a dormant 'primitive' society. This prevents one from recognizing that the tribals actually made use of Christianity to protect their cultural identity than Christianity subduing or deactivating them by way of impact. The tribals indeed valued the German missionaries as an expedient means for the restoration of their lost rights in the beginning. But soon, within two decades, they adopted and internalized Christianity in the tribal culture.[49]

## Resourcing Christianity for Reasoned Reconstruction

The integration of Christianity in the tribal culture reflected mainly in the social sphere. Christianity, the religion, had largely an imperfect hold over the tribal masses. The conversion, it should be recalled, was administered impromptu and on a large scale. Obviously most of the converts were neophytes and, within that, many were just nominal Christians. There were even cases of men calling themselves Christian as soon as they simply enrolled themselves as catechumen.[50] Yet, it is this tenuous adherence that the tribal leaders made adroit use of. In their various petitions to the government, they invariably introduced themselves as 12000 to 14000 'native Christians', no matter many had actually turned apostate. [51]

The tribal leaders employed Christianity so adopted not only to assert for immediate tribal rights, but also used it at a higher pedestal to contest the imposed concept of 'tribe' and construct a new one. Towards the last quarter of the nineteenth century, their status before the outsiders had become all-time low. Despised terms and phrases, that we have noted, were in popular use. Yet, the humanitarian attitude of the missionaries and a few individual European officials, leading to occasional recognition of the tribal rights and *bhuinhari* status in official discourse, encouraged them to reiterate their earlier status. The tribals based their claims on cultural and ethical grounds. In 1869, a Munda stated before E.T. Dalton, Commissioner of Chotanagpur : 'We consider Nagpore [Chotanagpur] our Gya, Ganga, Kasi and Prayag. The bones of our ancestors lie buried in the bowels of Nagpore. We are no colonialists from other countries, but derive race from Nagpore.'[52] This was rationalized further by claiming that 'other castes than us do not engage themselves to making the jungle clear'.[53]

With these convictions, as part of a broader effort of regaining their lost status, the tribals resorted to the resource of Christianity for refurbishment of the concept of indigenous 'tribe'. They drew analogy of their being *bhuinhars* with episodes of the Old Testament. That is how a group led by one 'John the Baptist', which has been mocked as 'ludicrously comic[al]'[54], named itself as the 'Children of Mael'.[55] Implicit in the assumption of these names was to describe the tribals as special people, like the 'chosen' Israelites. A letter from two former Munda students of the GEL mission school addressed to the mission authorities makes it explicit :

We Mundas used to have a patriarchal form of government. We gave taxes to the patriarchs (*makshays*), not rent for the land, but a religious type tax. Anyone, who reads Leviticus, chapter 25 [of the Old Testament] can understand the conditions of our people; they were similar to those of the Israelites....[56]

The leaders re-asserted the idea in a petition of 1881 to the government : 'We do not beg Your Majesty for a ... right [different] than that of the Israelites, who after wandering in the jungles, and suffering many trials became heir of the holy land....'[57] Christianity to the tribals, in short, became an advanced weapon to fight for a 'human' social status under a dignified term of tribe.

**Conclusion**

Tribes in Indian history have culturally been among the most suppressed people, both in pre-colonial and colonial settings, though in a greater degree in the latter phase. The nineteenth century colonial ethnography, in defining tribe, conceptually integrated it in the framework of the caste system. The tribes were placed, as a residue social group, at the bottom-most of the caste hierarchy, forming the 'Brahmanical opposite'.[58] From this conceptual understanding rose a number of specific terms, all increasingly despicable, on various tribal groups.

The close association of the conceptual making of this sort with colonialism and those terms coming into day-to-day public use has led scholars to see 'tribe' as a colonial creation.[59] What is blatantly ignored is that the colonial creators actually relied heavily upon pre-colonial, mainly Hindu, ideas and information on the subject. Colonialism, thus, simply revived the term and vulgarized it by injecting in it the factor of Social Darwinism and firmly fixing the tribes at the lowest stratum of the human civilization.

The term so raised has been almost static. This is because scholars are reluctant to take tribe as an independent unit of human progress under certain specific ecology; they stick to the belief of its being essentially a stage of human progress. Tribe is, thus, stereotyped or 'savaged', as R.C. Guha would like to call, on the basis of conventional understanding and data.[60] To nationalist India, the tribes became either 'tiresome savages' or 'colourful folks engaged in sexual orgies, human sacrifice and head-hunting'.[61] The factor assigned to such status was the tribals being 'inferior in mental capacity, military organization, material advancement and social efficiency'.[62]

While scholars recognize stereotyping, they lack the boldness of exploring varied and alternative, including tribal, sources for an objective understanding of the concept.[63] The failure remained the basic reason why the twentieth century nationalist effort to correct the concept did not work—whether the case was of coinage of a new term like *vanavasi,* or of the romantic move of according the tribe a *kshatriya* status or a 'civilized' label.[64]

As general attitude refused to be open minded, it is not surprising that the tribals themselves took the initiative for a respectable human term under cultural assertion in various periods of history. Thus, when the nationalist India of 1930s came up with the new terminology of *adimjati* (primitive), the Mundas and Uraons made their choice clear for *adivasi* (indigenous people).[65] In that sense, *adivasi* became a fought and won term of the tribals, as independent India accepted it in popular use.

But this did not liberate the term from the inherited bias. In independent India the *adivasi* officially became 'scheduled tribe' or *anusuchit janajati.* Notably, as a legacy of colonial ethnology, the word *jati* (caste) forms part of the official term. Meanwhile, the term *adivasi* acquired political ramifications, i.e. claim of first right by the local people over local resources, making its use contentious. That makes Government of India dither in accepting 'indigenous people', now a United Nations term for tribes, despite a suggestion from the UN.

## NOTES & REFERENCES

1. J. Hoffmann, *Encyclopaedia Mundarica,* Vol. IV, Patna, 1950, p. 1117.
2. The tribals addressed each other as 'horo', 'maleh' and so on that meant 'man'.
3. Indian Confederation of Indigenous and Tribal Peoples, Indigenous and Tribal Solidarity, New Delhi, 1997, p. 105.
4. K.S. Singh, Tribal Movements in India, Vol. I and II, New Delhi, 1986. In Chotanagpur the first revolt took place in 1789, closely following the actual occupation of the region in 1772.
5. 'Memorandum submitted by the Chotanagpur Improvement Society', *Report of the Indian Statutory Commission, Selections from Memoranda and Oral Evidence by Non-officials (Part I),* Calcutta, 1930, p. 447.
6. This is what cultural theoretician, Edward Said perceived in his *Orientalism,* New York, 1979. The view has since been critiqued by a host of writers. I take cue mainly from Andrew Porter, 'Cultural imperialism' and Protestant Missionary Enterprise 1780-1914', *Journal of Imperial and Commonwealth History,* Vol. 25, No. 3, September 1997.

7. The scholarly tendency in the context of the growth of the Jharkhand movement in late 1930s has been to discern tribal 'separatism' in Chotanagpur, chiefly 'sustained by continuous flow of external stimuli'. See P.G. Ganguli, 'Separatism in Indian Polity: A Case Study', M.C. Pradhan *et al.*, ed., *Anthropology and Archaeology : Essays in Honour of Verrier Elwin 1902-64,* London, 1969; K.S. Singh, 'Tribal Ethnicity in a Multi-ethnic Society: Conflict and Integration in Colonial and Post-colonial Chotanagpur', UNESCO, *Trends in Ethnic Group Relations in Asia and Oceania,* Paris, 1979.
8. J. Reid, *Final Report on the Survey and Settlement Operations in the Ranchi District, 1902-1910, Calcutta,* 1912, p. 22.
9. See, for instance, C.P.N. Sinha ed. *India Tracts : Major J. Browne's Report of Jungle Tarai People of South Bihar during 1774-1779,* Darbhanga, 1996; James Long, *Selections from Unpublished Records of Government for the Years 1748 to 1767,* second edition, Calcutta, 1973; Reginald Heber, *Narratives of a Journey Through the Upper Provinces India from Calcutta to Bombay 1824-25,* Vol. I, second edition, Delhi, 1985, p. 258.
10. British linguist of the late nineteenth and early twentieth century, G.A. Grierson sees the meaning of 'Kol' as dirty pig, which the tribals also believed.
11. Sinha, *India Tracts,* p. 15.
12. Report entitled "The Coles", *The Bengal Harkaru and Chronicle,* Calcutta, 24 February 1832, in J.C. Jha, *The Tribal Revolt* of Chotanagpur 1831-32, Patna, 1987, Appendix 2, p. 269.
13. J. Hoffmann, *Encyclopaedia Mundarica,* Vol. V, Patna, 1950, pp. 1449-50; *ibid.,* Vol. II, Patna, 1950, pp. 462; Letter dated 22 May from R.D. Haldar, Special Commissioner to Deputy Commissioner, Lohardugga, in Papers relating to Chotanagpur Agrarian Disputes, Vol. I, p. 82
14. The details of this movement is well documented in John MacDougall, *Land or Religion?: The Sardar and Kherwar Movements in Bihar 1858-1895,* New Delhi, 1985.
15. L.S.S. O'Malley, *Census of India, 1911,* Part I, Bengal, Bihar and Orissa, p. 234; Papers relating to Chotanagpur Agrarian Disputes, Vol. I, p. 82.
16. Romila Thapar, *Ancient Indian Social History,* New Delhi, 1978, pp. 152-92.
17. The latter phenomenon is explained more explicitly in case of the Gond tribes of central India. See W.G. Griffith, 'The Folklores of the Kols', *Man in India,* Vol. XXIV, No. 4; J. Forsyth, *The Highlands of Central India: Notes on their Forests, Wild Tribes, Natural History and Sports,* London, 1919. In Chotanagpur, it reflects abundantly

in the annals of the Nagabansis. See S.C. Roy 'An Abstract of the Annals of the Nagabansi Raj Family', *Man in India,* Vol. VIII, No. 4.

18. 'Srimati Satyawati Gaur Gahi Bakhni' (in *Kurukh, the dialect of the Uraons*), Dhumkuria, May-June, 1952, p. 10.
19. James Long, 'Report of the Sociological Section', Proceedings of the Transactions of the Bethune Society, Calcutta, 1870, p. 414.
20. *Ibid.*
21. M.G. Hallet, *Bihar and Orissa District Gazetteer: Ranchi,* Patna, 1917, p. 32.
22. Reid, *Final Report of the Survey and Settlement Operation of Ranchi,* p. 34.
23. S.C. Roy, 'Ethnological Investigation in Official Records' (Report of S.T. Cuthbert, 1827), *Journal of Bihar and Orissa Research Society* (JBORS), Vol. VII, Part 4, pp. 33-34 (hereafter 'Cuthbert Report, 1827'); S.C. Roy, 'Ethnological Investigation in Official Records', vol. XXI, Part 4, p. 243; H. Ricketts, *Selections from the Records of the Government of Bengal, No. XX,* Calcutta, 1855, p. 36; P.C. Roy Choudhury, *1857 in Bihar (Chotanagpur and Santhal Parganas),* second edition, Patna, p. 39; *Indo-European Correspondence,* 22 January 1890, p. 77.
24. F.A. Grignard, "The Oraons and Mundas : From the Times of their Settlement in India", *Anthropos,* Vol. IV, 1909. p. 7.
25. The sway of Darwinist racism was real. A Bavarian tourist in Chotanagpur in the early twentieth century remarked to his local host pointing at a Munda who was on the roadside: 'That fellow sitting there is either a monkey, and then I am a man,, or if he is a man, and then I am god'. J. Hoffmann, *Encyclopaedia Mundarica,* Vol. IV, p. 1117.
26. They came to be known as 'sadans', who constitute a sizeable community in the State of Jharkhand today.
27. Martin Orans, *The Santals : A Tribe in Search of Great Tradition,* Detroit, 1965.
28. B.B. Choudhuri, 'Society and Culture of the Tribal World in Colonial India: Reconsidering the Notion of "Hinduization" of Tribes', in Hetukar Jha ed. *Perspectives on Indian Society and History : A Critique,* New Delhi, 2002.
29. K.S. Singh, *Tribal Society in India,* New Delhi, 1985.
30. 'Memorandum submitted by the Chotanagpur Improvement Society', p. 447.
31. Anonymous, 'The Kols of Chota Nagpur', *Calcutta Review,* Vol. XLIX, No. XCVII, 1869, p. 140.
32. Roy, 'An Abstract of the Annals of the Nagabansi Raj Family', pp. 269-70.
33. *Ibid.*, p. 268.

34. 'Cuthbert Report, 1827', p. 5.
35. E.T. Dalton, *Descriptive Ethnology of Bengal*, Calcutta, 1872, 162-63.
36. S.C. Roy, *The Mundas and Their Country*, Bombay, 1970, p. 93.
37. *Ibid*.
38. Jha, *op. cit*., p. 259; Ganguli, *op. cit*., p. 100. A reflection of this theory is found in Myron Weiner, *Sons of the Soil: Migration and Ethnic Conflict in India*, Delhi, 1978, which sees 'passive protest' in the emigration of the displaced tribals vis-à-vis active protest in the form of revolts and movements. The emigrants actually left their land nostalgically, often with a resolve to get it back. Some of them did return with savings in hand and joined the *Sardari Larai*. Some others converted to Christianity in the migrated land to empower themselves. This indicates that emigration was not really passive exit.
39. Letter dated 22 December, 1871 from E.T. Dalton, Commissioner, Chotanagpur to Secretary, Revenue, Bengal, in Papers relating to Chotanagpur Agrarian Disputes, vol. I, p. 21.
40. Joseph Bara, 'Seeds of Mistrust : Tribal and Colonial Perspectives on Education in Chotanagpur, 1834-*c*.1850', *History of Education*, Vol. 34, No. 6.
41. See for detailed description of the circumstances in Joseph Bara, 'Colonialism, Christianity and the Tribes of Chhotanagpur in East India, 1845-1890', *South Asia*, Vol. XXX, No. 2.
42. This took place especially between 1855, when Henry Ricketts, visiting Member, Board of Revenue, prepared a report and 1880, when R.D. Haldar, Special Commissioner to the *bhuinhari* survey submitted his report. Haldar's note entitled 'An account of the village system of Chotanagpur', appended to the main report, especially became an authoritative reference material on the subject of *bhuinhari*.
43. Scholars have either overlooked this movement or have failed to recognize its importance. In the entire set of 'Subaltern Studies' of the Oxford University Press, the subject is unattended. K.S. Singh, whose scholarship on tribal movement of Chotanagpur is well-known for over three decades, is more concerned to see how Birsa movement was an 'advance' over this movement and assigns latter the role of a second fiddle; see his *Birsa Munda and his Movement 1874-1901 : A Study of a Millennarian Movement in Chotanagpur*, Calcutta, 1983. Historian, Sumit Sarkar in his authoritative survey of popular movements in colonial India explains the 'primary resistance' led by traditional chiefs in Chhotanagpur before this movement and the 'revivalist' movement led by Birsa following it, but skips comment on *Sardari Larai*; see Sumit Sarkar, *Popular Movement and "Middle Class" Leadership in late Colonial India: Perspective from below*, Calcutta, 1983.

44. Petition dated 25 March, 1879 of '14000 Christians' to the Commissioner of Chota Nagpur, in Roy, *The Mundas and Their Country*, pp. 162-63.
45. MacDougall, *Land or Religion?*
46. A tribal saying is *'Topi topi ek topi'*, which means that donning whitemen, whether a colonial official or a missionary, were the same.
47. Some see Christianity playing the role of a mere 'catalyst' in the tribal society where chief role was played by market forces, giving rise to a 'well-off' tribal peasantry. See Romila Thapar and M.H. Siddiqi, 'Chotanagpur: The Pre-colonial and Colonial Situation', in UNESCO, *Trends in Ethnic Group Relations in Asia and Oceania*, Paris, 1979, p. 39. Others discern a direct role of it. See especially Roy, *The Mundas and Their Country*.
48. K.S. Singh, for instance, finds a proactive working of Christianity which 'radiated deeper' into the tribal society and raised a band of 'reactionary' tribal leaders. See Singh, *Birsa Munda and his Movement*, p. 20.
49. For a picture of it from contemporary writings see, Joseph Mullens, *Ten Years of Missionary Labour in India between 1852 and 1861*, London, 1863, p. 43.
50. W.W. Hunter, *Statistical Account of Bengal:* The Districts of Ranchi and Lohardaga, Vol. XVI, reprint, Delhi, 1976, p. 443.
51. Report of the GEL Mission for the year 1874, quoted in *ibid.*, p. 436.
52. Quoted by R.D. Haldar in his 'An Account of Village System of Chotanagpur', appended to Resolution dated 25 November 1880 of the Government of Bengal on the Report of the Special Commissioners, in Papers relating to Chotanagpur Agrarian Disputes, Vol. I, p. 103.
53. Petition to the Lt. Governor of Bengal, 1881, in MacDougall, *Land or Religion*, Appendix B3, p. 261.
54. Roy, *The Mundas and Their Country*, p. 163.
55. Letter dated 19 November, 1887 from Stevens to Chief Secretary, Bengal.
56. Undated (but dating some time before 1887) petition by two former students of the Lutheran Mission School, in John MacDougall, *Land or Religion?*, Appendix B2, p. 261.
57. Petition dated 1881 to the Lt. Governor of Bengal, in *ibid.*, p. 262.
58. Crispin Bates, 'Race, Caste and Tribe in Central India: The Early Origins of Indian Anthropometry' in Peter Robb (ed.), *The Concept of Race in South Asia*, Delhi, 1995.
59. Among many works on the subject, see specifically on the Jharkhand tribes, Susana B.C. Devalle, *Discourses of Ethnicity : Culture and Protest in Jharkhand*, New Delhi, 1992.

60. R.C. Guha, *Savaging the Civilized;* Verrier Elwin, *His Tribals and India*, Delhi, 1997.
61. Verrier Elwin, *The Tribal World of Verrier Elwin: An Autobiography*, Delhi, 1964, p. 290.
62. L.S.S. O'Malley, *Modern India and the West: A Study of the Interaction of Civilizations*, London, 1941, p. 726.
63. *Indian Historical Review* (Vol. XXXIII, No. 1, January 2006) devoted to the theme 'Adivasis in Colonial India'. A number of essays in this issue deal with 'construction' of 'tribe' and 'Adivasi'.
64. The term 'vanavasi' was conceived, in early 1950s, by Adimjati Seva Mandal, a nationalist non-governmental organization engaged in welfare works among the tribal populations. The idea of 'kshatriya' status was floated on the eve of independence by some philanthropists; see Verrier Elwin, Foreword (written in 1944) to All-India Arya (Hindu) Dharma Sewa Sangha, *Religious Banditry*, Delhi, undated, p. 15. As for the tribals being called 'civilized', see Elwin, *The Tribal World of Verrier Elwin*.
65. The tribals formed a political organization called Adivasi Sabha, the forerunner of Jharkhand Party and published an organ '*Adivasi*' since 1938.

# 8

# Socio-religious Movements and the Evolution of Religious Identity among the *Adivasis* of Jharkhand

PADMAJA SEN

## Introduction

The socio-religious movements of the major *adivasi*[1] communities of Jharkhand under review, namely the Munda, Santal, Ho and Oraon, took place during nineteenth and twentieth centuries. More prominent among them were the Kherwar movement of Santals, Birsa movement of Mundas, Tana Bhagat movement of Oraons, *Satya* or *Punya Dharam* and Haribaba movements of Hos. These movements have so far been studied from anthropological, historical and politico-sociological angles.[2] The purpose of such studies has mainly been to highlight the prevailing socio-economic and political situations. These generally glossed over the religious content of the movements supposedly as an ancillary to the articulation of autonomous political identity by the indigenes. Naturally these broached the religious data of the movements, without being much concerned about their specific religious nature and significance.

An approach to religion as an epiphenomenon of social, political, psychological or cultural structures logically results into the tendency of ignoring the uniqueness of religious beliefs. My study of the literature of the socio-religious movements of

Jharkhand has convinced me that the religious content of the movements has either been ignored as trifle and insignificant or overshadowed by the socio-economic and political moorings. At best the content has been explained as a means and symbol of indigenous solidarity and as expression of their identity in the face of existential crises and invading cultures. The lack of appreciation of the essentially religious nature of the data and their philosophical import has resulted in the repetition of information time and again without a meaningful discourse on them.

It may be agreed that 'religion is a social phenomenon' and social facts determine the forms of religion to some extent in a society. But they cannot fully account for the core of religion, its origin, function and meaning.[3] We also cannot deny that the religious facts are deeply rooted in our religious experience. As such the central notions of religion are essentially religious in nature and should deserve an independent status. I draw support from Evans-Pritchard's observation about the Nuer religion : 'that Nuer religious thought and practices are influenced by their whole social life is evident from our study of them . . . But Nuer conceptions of God cannot be reduced to or explained by social order' to substantiate that Nuer belief in *Kwoth* or spirit is an intuitive apprehension.[4] Smart echoes a similar view in the following passage 'many central beliefs and practices in religion are autonomous, in the sense that they are not simply to be explained in terms of social function . . . this sense implies that there are religious motives or reasons for holding beliefs and performing rituals.'[5]

The chapter therefore argues that instead of reducing the religious content of the socio-religious movements to a mere expression of the assertion of autonomous political identity of the indigenes of Jharkhand it should be studied in its own right as an important stage of their belief system. In view of the recently growing concern among the *adivasis* of Jharkhand for claiming themselves as a distinct religious community represented by *Sarna Dharam* the above religious content of the movements has acquired a new meaning. I presume that the religious tenets of the movements are not separate and unrelated phenomena, rather these signify a natural evolution of an organic belief system leading to a wider and more integrated phase known as *Sarna Dharam*. A diachronic and synchronic study of these data in relation to early and the present form of their faith with a focus on their specific religious character may help us apprehend the underlying logical structure of their belief system as a basis of this identity-claim. My central concern here would be to develop an understanding of the religious data in its individuality and particularity. At the same time in order to appreciate their real significance and meaning they need to be reinterpreted in the light of the logical structure of *adivasi* belief system.

## Pre-Movement Overview of *Adivasi* Religion

Before initiating a discussion I consider it necessary to clarify two points. First, the *adivasis* of Jharkhand belonged till recently[6] to a dialect-based society. So we do not have a fund of indigenous literature to reconstruct a systematic knowledge about their past belief system. But the available information indicates that they have had a rich religious tradition. We have, therefore, more or less to draw on exotic source [7] for this task. Second, I have studied the belief systems of the major *adivasi* groups in one cluster namely *adivasi* religion as an organic whole. This has been done on the basis of the understanding that in spite of some minor differences and also difference in names of the deities there is a broad agreement in their nature and offerings made to them as well as the mode of prayers. Their doctrinal schemes[8] and religious sensibilities also exhibit similarity in major concerns.[9]

The Census Reports of 1901 and 1911 classified the indigenes as animists. We know that they believed in natural objects as symbolically representing spirits. Though supposedly residing in natural objects the spirits can also transcend their spatial locus at their will. This suggests that their religion was closer to spiritism and naturalistic religion rather than animism.

The doctrinal scheme of the *adivasi* faith suggests a variety of religious propositions namely, those concerning a Supreme deity, as the creator, destroyer and sustainer of the world, those dealing with the pantheon of benevolent and malevolent invisible mysterious objects of worship and those related to the process of worship i.e. the prayers and propitiations. A detailed study of the scheme provides an insight into the mutual and organic relationship between their beliefs, myths, rituals and practices that embody the key structure and basic elements of their faith. I now provide relevant details[10] to structure the pre-movement *adivasi* religious ambience to identify the areas of conformity and departure during later religious movements.

## The Notion of Supreme Being

The *adivasi* myths[11] profess the notion of godhead as the creator, preserver and destroyer. They presuppose the existence of a *causa sui* Supreme Creator.[12] Different names are used for Him. Mundas and Hos called Him *Singbonga,* while Santals addressed Him variously as *Thakur, Thakur Jiu, Cando* and *Singbonga*. On the other hand Oraons named Him as *Dharmi* or *Dharmes*. According to Roy[13] this was a recent accretion, which replaced the original name of *Biri-Belas* or Sun Lord. They also used the Hindu name of *Bhagwan* to denote *Dharmes*. With minor variations the myths narrate how God created this universe, man and animals. He was believed to be not only the creator but at the same time also the preserver and the destroyer.[14] He preserved His creation from the mythic horse. The stress on procreation, through the induction of rice-beer, also suggested His eagerness to preserve the creation. He was conceived as the protector of total welfare and the cause of all actions in their lives. The destruction of creation with rain of fire revealed His aspect of destroyer. However, destruction was not His ultimate purpose. So one pair was saved, from whom the world was peopled again[15]. Here the similarity with such other Grand Traditions as Hinduism and Christianity is evident.

Originally Mundas, Hos and Santals conceived Him as a personal God around the centrality of whom their religious beliefs continued to rotate. The Supreme Being was conceived as the guardian of the entire tribe. He was likened to a father who also chastised when the children erred. Attached to this was the belief that the social order that God had created had to follow the basic norms, a departure from which would invite divine-ordained suffering, rather destruction, in lived life itself. *Adivasis* had a distinct mode of worship for the Supreme Being. They expressed their gratitude to Him through elaborate system of prayer and propitiation. They sought the blessings of *Singbonga* before every religious ceremony for the welfare of the family. His services were invoked to avert sickness or drought or famine particularly when the prayer to the minor deities failed. Offerings and libations were made to Him in the form of a goat or white cock or a morsel of food or a few drops of water.

## The Pantheon

Besides a belief in *Singbonga* the Supreme God, belief in a pantheon characterized as the *Adivasi* religion. Through an interaction with their natural environment they developed their indigenous cults both out of emotive and intellectual reasons. They believed in the dichotomy of the good and evil forces. For them supernatural world was ruled respectively by a pantheon of benevolent and malevolent deities and spirits. They recognized evil as a necessary fact, which can never be fully wiped out. So they made no attempt to justify evil as is done in more developed theistic religions. Instead an absolute duality of benevolent and malevolent spirits was accepted. They maintained that the above forces, in which human agencies were incapable of playing any role, essentially determined their lives. So it was natural that they always sought the blessings of the benevolent deities through worship and warded off the anger of the malevolent spirits through propitiation. Mundas named them respectively as *Banita* and *Manita Bongas*. Originally Oraons believed in the beneficence of all their spirits. But due to the contact with grand traditions, they began investing benevolent nature to some of them only. At the same time they evolved a mischievous class of the tramp or stray spirits as *Mua, Malech, Churel* and *Satbahini*. Their malevolent world also included the notions of 'evil eye' (*najar*) and 'evil mouth' (*baibhak*) or 'evil touch' (*chhut*).

The pantheon was evolutionary in nature and a multi-tiered one, serving as general and special guardians to conduct their total welfare at individual/familial and community levels. They generally believed in the ancestral spirits as protecting the welfare of all living family members. This seems to emanate from the faith in the eternity of self or *Ji*. They believed that the departed soul continued to live with the family in the form of spirit or shadow forever. They had then their village deities looking after the welfare of villages. Some of the *Adivasi* groups had also deities to serve their *khunt* or sub-clan interests. There was yet the notion of group of gods and spirits like *Chandi* as the special deity for the Oraon bachelors and *Acharel* for women. Besides the above they also reposed faith in the spirits of nature. So the nature-gods frequently appear in myths. According to Ho myth *Nage-era* (river goddess) saved two souls under a vast sheet of water. Other than *Nage-era, Maran Buru* (mountain god), *Jaher-era* (the lady of the sacred grove) and the Asur women whom *Singbonga* had turned into the *bongas* of nature also appear in myths.

Elaborate rituals were performed to worship and propitiate deities and spirits. They offered morsel of food, fowl, sheep, goat, pig, rice beer, fruits etc., depending upon socially specific norms of religious practices. They gradually inducted the institution of priesthood to mediate between worshippers and worshipped. These facts make it clear that welfare in the present world had been major concern for the *adivasis*. But at the same time the faith in a Supreme God is ample indication of their religious intentions. *Dharmi* or *Dharmes* was held as the Holy One, manifest in the Sun, a perfectly pure, beneficent being. He was the head of the pantheon. He was supposed to be the lord of other deities who held their positions and performed their duties due to Him. But the evolving nature of their belief around Him becomes evident from the information given by Dalton. Dalton wrote about the Oraon belief in the helplessness of *Dharmes* before the spirit of evil leading to their subsequent adoration of malignant spirits more than Him. But a few decades later we learn from Roy[16] about the restoration of *Dharmes* to the apex of the Oraon pantheon as against His comparative insignificance a few decades back during Dalton's time.

Over centuries *adivasi* religious faith tended to be syncretic, gradually imbibing deities and spirits from other indigenous groups as well as Hindu neighbours. Whether this syncretism was inspired by a desire for revitalizing their spiritual life or not is not clear. It appears to have been done with a utilitarian motive that the exotic elements would come to their rescue when their own deities fail. Oraons maintained that except *Dharmes* all their spirits and deities had an exotic origin. Their *Devi Mai* and *Mahadev* had been inducted from Hindus. *Barnda Pachcho,* a household *bhut,* was in fact of Munda origin. Similarly Oraon custom of putting up *pulkhis* or memorials showed the Munda influence. On the other hand from the Hindus they had imbibed the practice of throwing charred bones of the dead into streams or pool of water. The Santals had inducted *Kali, Durga, Ganga, Laksmi, Ram* and *Mahadev* from the Hindus. This syncretism seems to be a timeless feature of *Adivasi* belief system continuing through their revivalist movement. This will be elaborated in the next section of this essay.

## Other Features

*Adivasis* of Jharkhand did not raise temples for their deities. But it was common of them to demarcate a part of the primordial forest or *sal* grove adjacent to the village as their place of worship. Mundas and Munda-speaking tribes like Santals and Hos had also a sacred precinct in their houses called *Ading* or *Bhitar* as the abode of their household deities. Moreover, Oraons built *Devi-sthan* or *Devi-Manda* or altar for *Devimai* and *Mahadev-manda* or *Mahadev-sthan* for *Mahadev.*

Generally speaking *adivasis* did not practice idolatry. But they often attributed form and personality to their supernatural entities. I cite a few instances to substantiate this point. For an Oraon *Chala Pachcho* or *Sarna Burhia* was personified by an old woman with matted locks of snow-white hair. *Chandi*, the goddess of hunting, was believed to be capable of assuming any shape she liked. Oraons also used stone as symbols of their deities and wooden *khuntas* or pegs as seats of ghosts or human spirits. Small clay cones represented their *Devimai*. Santals used stones to represent their village spirits. This may be identified as the beginning of a trend towards idol worship.

We notice differences in the mode of worship as well as changes creeping into their faith.[17] The accretions may be linked to the impact of changed spatio-temporal settings. Obviously the belief system did not seem to have gained the maturity as to pose such contemplative question viz. what were the evidences for and against the truth of its religious claims. The questions seeking rational justification for ancestor worship, propitiation of malevolent spirits and so forth did not seem to be generally raised. But evidently the beliefs and practices were the symbolic expressions of their religious experience. They had their own reasons and grounds in such experience.

## Socio-Religious Movements

The major socio-religious movements as mentioned earlier are Birsa,[18] Kherwar,[19] Tana Bhagat[20] and *Satya* or *Punya Dharam*[21] and Haribaba movement.[22] The historical setting of the movement had a close bearing on them. History relates that *adivasis* cleared forests to found their villages. But under local kings as well as colonial rule they were deprived of their hearths and homes. Along with this their society was shaken 'to its roots' disrupting their old ways and traditional value system due to the invasion of the outsiders. Gradually they lost faith in their *Bongas* and their priests whom they found to be incapable of saving them from potent dangers. They were instead drawn towards Hinduism and Christianity for support. But this centripetal trend[23] had a deeper motive behind it.

Jharkhand *adivasis* had been subjected to an itinerant life for their survival both against natural odds and invading cultures. This created a constant crisis of identity. They sought to address this problem by evolving their material and moral culture as distinct from other cultural groups living in the neighbourhood. But at the same time they also selectively imbibed from grand traditions to meet the existential challenges. Kherwars and Birsa both seem to considerably model their system of beliefs and practices as well as an ethical code of conduct on Hinduism and Christianity.

The religious tenets of the movements may be summarized under the notions of the One Supreme Being, devotion, rejection of the pantheon, incarnation and the ethical codes. Central to their religious sensibility was the emphasis on One Personal God. Birsa preached that to this One God alone worship was due. For the Kherwars this God was the Hindu deity Ram. He was identified with Santal God *Cando*, the God of the universe. They insisted that originally they were the worshippers of One God alone, the departure from this, they imputed, was the cause of their present suffering. Tana Bhagats and *Satya* or *Punya Dharam* also asserted faith in One God. For Tana Bhagats He was *Dharmes*, their traditional personal God. But for *Satya* or *Punya Dharam* He was *Sat Malik* or True God who is invisible and omnipotent. It enjoined its adherents to stop image worship. We also notice the trend of exclusive tenets of particular movements. Tana Bhagats and Haribabites insisted on the path of devotion and meditation.

The faith in monotheism was logically strengthened by the rejection of the entire pantheon of *Bongas* and the practice of making offerings to propitiate them. Tana Bhagats preached abstention from the belief in *Bongas* and minor spirits and *bhuts*. Birsa declared :

*'O Spirits of hills, deep water,*
*You shall not get any (sacrifice) from us*
*You have not created earth and heaven,*
*Therefore, O Spirits, keep away.*[24]

A shift from the original belief system occurred when Birsa and others professed the concept of incarnation or *avtarvad*. Birsites believed that the faith in Birsa, the messenger of God, and prayers to him instead of propitiation of spirits, was the means of happiness. This faith later inspired them to turn their *Dharti Aba* (the Father of the Earth) i.e., Birsa himself, into God. This concept may be likened to the New King of Christianity. Another significant innovation was the warning that those not abiding by the above preaching of Birsa must face destruction. Suggestively the imposition of the omnipotence of God, capable of saving his devotees with miraculous powers as well as destroying them, upon the incarnate took Birsa closer to original mythic notion of Supreme Being.

The stress on the observance of a strict ethical code as a means to the total revival of *adivasi* life, both mundane and religious, is very obvious. Kherwars and Birsa preached vegetarianism, personal purification and temperance. Perhaps modelled on the Ten Commandments, Birsa prescribed a code of morals : use sacred thread like the Hindus, obey and show respect to parents and elders, love all creatures, practice a life of plain living and high thinking, remain united, observe a weekly holiday as a respite from work and devote the day in worship and meditation, do not lie, thieve, deceive or murder as they are sinful acts, do not practice inter-dining and marry Christian boys and girls and do not practice polygamy.

Vegetarianism, temperance, and personal purification through daily bath were the important tenets stressed by *Satya* or *Punya Dharam* also. Haribabites exhorted wearing of sacred thread and avoidance of vaccination and medicine.

The lack of uniformity in their items of reform is, however, very significant. It probably underlines the ideological disorientation of *adivasis* due to the stress created by moral and material degeneration under British rule.

## Towards an Understanding of the Religious Import of the Movements

We find that the movements were the expression of the inner tension and turmoil within the *adivasi* society not only at socio-economic and political levels but also at the level of religious beliefs. Other than socio-economic and political, one of the objectives of these movements was to revitalize indigenous belief systems. One cannot deny that many of the religious tenets of their movements were the result of the prevailing socio-economic and political conditions. To exemplify, Tana Bhagat preached : do not yoke cows and bullocks as they are sacred, give up modern mode of cultivation and relapse into traditional mode of shifting cultivation, do not serve as coolies and labourers under zamindars and non-Oraons, invoke the services of Birsa or German Kaiser (Wilhelm II) and Gandhi.

Similarly an emphasis on wearing sacred thread, purification and vegetarianism may certainly be interpreted as a movement towards sanskritization to attain a higher social status due to Hindu influence. These may also be a mark of distinction from the adherents of traditional *adivasi* beliefs. Likewise induction of the concept of incarnation by Birsa was due to the Hindu and Christian influence on him. Rejection of the propitiation of traditional pantheon is generally ascribed to their disillusionment of the *Bongas* due to their supposed inability to protect them in their existential crisis. Rejection of priesthood and animal sacrifice may have some economic implications. Induction of clear ethical code and prohibition of witchcraft, alcoholism and other superstitions may be for the moral and material well-being of their fellow people. In fact, such formulations may be understood as a significant tool for asserting *adivasi* solidarity against invading cultures. But the essentially religious of all these tenets are first the belief in a Supreme Being, which is central to their doctrinal scheme. Second is a growing sense of dependence and devotion at personal level toward Him to introduce an element of personal relationship between the worshipper and the worshipped in their belief system.[25]

The religious significance of the movements may be better appreciated if we analyze their religious content in the context of the early beliefs. A shift in the religious beliefs during movements as compared to the early faith is very obvious. The rejection of the propitiation of pantheon, priesthood and animal sacrifice, emphasis on specific purification, vegetarianism, and introduction of the concepts of incarnation as well as devotion and prayers at personal level are clearly opposed to their traditional faith. These create a doubt over the necessary link between the movements and the early *adivasi* faith. It formed an impression that the leaders of the movement had deviated from the original belief system and had preached altogether a distinct mode of worship. This has perhaps been one of the reasons of gradual decline in the earlier popularity of Birsaism or the Bhagat or other cults. But it may be suggested here that such shifts may occur within an organic belief system on account of some inner tension. For example, the rejection of the pantheon, which can also be interpreted as a movement from polytheism to monotheism may be ascribed to the tension creeping in the system due to the Christian influence.[26] The major sources of the inner tension may be ascribed to the meeting of the received faith and modern values. It will not be irrelevant to point out that the religious reforms in Hinduism have been explained in this line.

In spite of the above differences traces of mutual and organic interrelation between the earlier faith and religious movements are evident. Since the movements were aimed at social and religious reforms many trifle and peripheral aspects of original beliefs have been renounced in the process. But a fundamental belief in a Supreme Personal Being forms the basis for a strong link between the two. The Supreme Being of the religious movements has variously been identified with the traditional deity. Thus in spite of advocating different modes of worship the Kherwars identify the Supreme Being with the Hindu deity Ram as well as Santal God *Chando*. The same *Chando* is again conceived as holy trinity after the Christian faith and the Lord Vishnu, the god of preservation of the Hindus of whom Ram is regarded as an incarnation. A song composed by Bhagirath expresses the idea thus :

*He is . . . .*
*The Three Cando, one Cando . . . .*
*He is the Ram Cando of the kings,*
*The wheel (i.e. round) Cando of mankind.*[27]

The word wheel in the above verse has been interpreted as the *cakra* of Vishnu. For Tana Bhagats He is *Dharmes* and for *Satya* or *Punya Dharam*, the True God. Whether Birsa's notion of Supreme Being is the same as *Singbonga* or not is debatable. According to Sinha He was *Singbonga*. But Singh argues that Birsa had disowned *Singbonga* and preached the concept of the fatherhood of God or *Aba*. However, he also accepts that the denunciation of *Singbonga* is only implied. [28] The concept of the Supreme Being has also evolved through the movements. In the earlier faith He is conceived as the creator, preserver and destroyer of the world as well as the head of the pantheon. During the movements this notion crystallized into the monotheistic concept of Personal God who is the object of devotion.

Thus, we find that the *adivasis* were anxious to evolve a more dynamic belief system in view of the new religious elements creeping in their faith due to their interaction with the grand traditions active in this region. They were selectively imbibing new elements from the grand traditions with a view to revitalizing as well as reinterpreting their own belief system. But in this regard what Troisi writes about the Santals may be said to be true of other ethnic groups also :

> 'The adoption of both Hindu and Christian practices, however, did not change the basic characteristics of Santal religion. What the Santals aimed at was not to convert to Hinduism or to Christianity but to strike out new lines of their own, building on the part of their old beliefs taking something from the one and something else from the other.'[29]

In the process they were also attempting at conceptualizing and crystallizing the central concept of the Supreme Being of their original faith. However, it must be admitted that the conceptualization was at a very premature stage. These were the vital developments in the sense that they created the religious awareness, which led them ultimately to a conscious attempt of reconstructing their own religious tradition around *Sarna Dharam* as well as asserting their distinct indigenous religious identity.

## Evolution of Indigenous Religious Identity around *Sarna Dharam*

Contemporary trend among the *adivasis* is to identify themselves as *Sarna* that is believed to be self-sprung along with the creation itself, justifying its claim to be *Adi* or Eternal religion.[30] As we can see adopting the term *Sarna* to denote the religious belief system of *adivasis* is very significant. On the one hand, it is expressive of their closeness to nature, while on the other hand it also indicates their separate and independent religious identity. Historically speaking this assertion of distinct religious identity was coeval with their articulation of linguistic[31] and political identities. What seems crucial is that assertion of religious identity came in the wake of political assertions following the revival of the *Chotanagpur Improvement Society* in 1920 and the placing of the demand for a separate state for the *Adivasis* living in Bengal, Bihar and Orissa before the Simon Commission in 1928.[32]

There is a history behind adopting the term *Sarna* to denote their religion for which there was no specific common term earlier.[33] In 1932, the *adivasis* of Chotanagpur held a conference at Chaibasa of delegates from Bihar, Bengal and Orissa. Delegates resolved to use the name *Sarna Dharam* to specify their ancient religion. Raghunath Murmu or *Guru Gomke* (esteemed Guru) founded *Sarna Dharam Sembet* i.e. Sacred Grove Religion Organisation. Its avowed objective was to express solidarity of the *adivsis* around *Sarna Dharam* and to restore them to their traditional faith. The Hos of Singhbhum founded *Dupub Samaj*, an association professing faith in *Dupub Dharam*, the name they chose for *Sarna Dharam*. Similarly the Oraons established *Sarna Navayuvak Sangha*. The *All-India Sarna Association* came up in 1978 to preserve and develop *adivasi* culture and religion. However, the term *Sarna* has not yet been consolidated to be the only expression for a composite *adivasi* religion by rationalizing existing differences in pantheon and practices. Moreover, several other words like *Adi Dharam, adivasi* or *Janjati Dharam, Sari Dharam, Dupub Dharam, Sansari Dharam, Jahera Dharam, Bongaism* etc. are used as synonyms. However the term *Sarna* is the most popular one widely accepted representation of their faith. Notwithstanding the varied use of terms what becomes clear is that the *adivasis* are bent on asserting themselves as an independent religious community. This assertion of religious identity around *Sarna Dharam* is a natural development from the original faith itself.

The recent form of *adivasi* religion redefines their original faith. Despite the polytheistic attitude prevalent among Jharkhand *Adivasis Sarna Dharam* emphasizes One Supreme God[34] designated as *Singbonga, Dharmes* or *Haram*? This faith in a personal God is akin to the monotheistic trait of the *Adivasi* movements. In fact the belief in a Supreme God forges the strong link between earlier faith, the movements and the *Sarna Dharam*. The relation between God and man has been conceived here at once as a direct and very intimate one. This notion again is the legacy of the past. The recent trend is to emphasize the affectionate relation between grandparent and grand children. It seems to be a reinterpretation of the original belief in the strong bond between *Singbonga*, the father, and the *Adivasis*, the son. Even in its reinterpreted form the idea of direct and affectionate relationship between the worshipper and worshipped is very pronounced. It combines on the one hand a direct relation between man and the Supreme Being of the original faith and on the other the element of devotion of the movements. Man has a free access to God. The mediation of a priest is not considered necessary. Here adherents of *Sarna Dharam*, like Kherwarism and Birsaism, offer a challenge to the mediatory role of the priests, which had crept into their belief system.

An important link with their original faith is also expressed in their belief in the eternity of self or *Ji*. The self, according to *Sarna*, survives death. But they neither believe in rebirth nor in heaven or hell. For them the act, which is socially approved, is considered meritorious and that which is disapproved by the society is sin. The soul does not go to heaven or hell after death. But it ever remains with the family in the *Ading* or *Bhitar*. It does not believe in *Avatar*, Messiah or *Paigambar*. Thus it distances itself from the established religions as well as Birsa cult.

Other important features and its link with the original faith may be summed up briefly. It does not believe in erecting temples, churches or mosques as places of worship. Natural objects like forests, hills and rivers are considered to be the best abode of gods and spirits. This underlines a conscious attempt both to forge a distance from other religions and accretions that had crept into their faith in its pre-reformatory stage. This also signifies their notion of tribe-nature-continuum, the most remarkable feature of *Sarna Dharam*. Nature is considered sacred and man is essentially dependent on it but he has no right to control it. This is an innovative interpretation of *adivasis* faith, which has not been insisted upon by earlier religious reformers. One may identify the expression of their faith in closeness to nature in their concept of *Sarna*. Originally the term *Sarna* stands for the sacred grove consisting of *sal* trees (*Shorea robusta*) adjacent to every *adivasi* village. As the abode of the spirits of nature it is associated with their religious practices.

However, at this stage the faith lacks a rational theorization and established norms. But like any other living religion *Sarna Dharam* is also dynamic and is ever in the process of evolving. According to the demands of socio-religious consciousness new elements are being gradually incorporated into it through various movements. It shares some of the common characteristics of religious traditions. Its doctrinal scheme is pregnant with the principles of closely knit beliefs and practices, cosmogony, call for dedicated commitment, moral code and an eschatological orientation. Like any religion it is also neither verifiable nor falsifiable. Above all it is dynamic and evolutionary. Though it is a religion of a particular ethnic group, *Sarna Dharam* also refers Truth in a way peculiarly suited to the indigenous temperament.

## Conclusion

Thus this chapter argues that the entire gamut of socio-religious movement, conventionally incorporated within indigenous identity movement, should not be approached merely as a strategy to attain a secular goal. Parallel to the claim of a distinct religious identity a student of the philosophy of religion, may also discern within the whole scheme a conscious attempt to evolve the religious beliefs and practices of the *adivasis* of Jharkhand around *Sarna Dharam*. Over centuries they evolved their own faith, which was different in many ways from that of the grand traditions. While doing so they selectively imbibed the beliefs and practices of the latter. But threatened by invading grand traditions they strove to revitalize their belief systems. This was marked by the two-fold strategy. On the one hand they continued to reiterate their faith in the acculturating tradition. But on the other the fear of being subsumed by grand traditions as well as the realization that adoption of exotic ways would only inadequately solve their mundane problems they seemed to chart a more assertive course. In the recent past this manifested in the conscious attempt to rebuild their religious tradition around *Sarna Dharam*.

Incorporating religious notions from the grand traditions may *prima facie* appear to be a lack of faith in their own belief system and institutions as well as a mark of absence of identity consciousness. But in reality this was the way the *adivasis* had collectively and consciously imbibed from other cultures whenever they had encountered any existentialist crisis. This acculturation was both selective and adaptive after which they continued to pursue their own faith.[35] In more recent times the method of articulation appeared to change when they pinned faith in their own religion and asserted their identity around *Sarna Dharam*. The feature of this assertion is to project the religious identity not in terms of single *adivasi* community but the entire gamut of Jharkhand *adivasi* society. This is at once a claim for what they are religiously that is *Sarna*, and what they are not that is a Hindu, Christian or a Muslim. In search of their distinct ethnic identity the educated *adivasis* are more and more inclined to their indigenous religious heritage. But this recall is more a reinterpretation than exact reproduction of their tradition.

**NOTES**

1. Indian tribes are denoted by such terms as tribals, *adivasis*, aboriginals, indigenes etc. But for this essay *adivasis* and indigenes have been chosen conforming to the preference made by tribals themselves to it to signify their being the original people.
2. S.P. Sinha, *Life and Times of Birsa Bhagwan*, Bihar Tribal Research Institute, (Ranchi, 1964); *Conflict and Tension in Tribal Society*, Concept Publishing Company, (New Delhi, 1993); S.C. Roy, *The Mundas and their Country*, Asia Publishing House, (Bombay, 1970.) and *Oraon Religion and Customs*, Editions Indian, (Calcutta, 1972); K.S. Singh, *Birsa Munda and His Movement* 1874-1901, Oxford University Press, (Calcutta, 1983); M. Areeparampil, 'Socio-Cultural and Religious Movements among the Ho Tribals of Singhbhum district of Bihar' in M. Miri (ed.) *Continuity and Change in Tribal Society*, Indian Institute of Advanced Study, (Shimla, 1993); S. Fuchs, *Rebellious Prophets*, Asia Publishing House, (Bombay, 1965), Philip Ekka, Tribal Movements, Tribal Research and Documentation Centre (TRDC), (Chhattisgarh, 2003); P. Sen and A.K. Sen, 'Religion as Identity: Evolution of Religious Ideas among the Adivasis of Jharkhand' (Jointly) Special Issue: Philosophical Traditions in the Indian Languages, *Journal of Indian Council of Philosophical Research*, (New Delhi, 2002).
3. While criticizing sociological theories of primitive religion Evans-Pritchard rightly observes, 'I certainly do not deny that religious ideas and practices are directly associated with social groups . . . What I do deny is that it is explained by any of these facts, or all of them together . . .' According to him we have to account for religious facts in terms of the totality of culture and society in which they are found. They must be understood as interrelated parts within a coherent system, which again gains meaning only as a part of a wider set of relations, E.E. Evans-Pritchard, *Theories of Primitive Religion*, Oxford University Press, London, 1965, p. 111-12.
4. Cited in N. Smart, *Concept and Empathy*, New York University Press, New York, 1986, pp. 187, 194.
5. *Ibid.*, p. 185.

6. To exemplify Santal and Ho communities have developed respectively *Olchiki and Waran Kshiti* scripts to earn the status of a literate society.
7. E.T. Dalton, *Tribal History of Eastern India,* Cosmo Publication, (Delhi, 1973), pp. 161-217, 245-262; Roy, *The Mundas,* pp. 221-222, 235, 266- 278, 328, 339 and *Oraon Religion and Customs,* pp. 11-82; D.N. Majumdar, *A Tribe in Transition,* Longmans Green & Co. Ltd., (Calcutta, 1937), pp. 126-143; A. Van Exem, *The Religious System of the Munda Tribe,* (Haus Volker, 1982), pp. 9-140; J. Troisi, *Tribal Religion(Religious Beliefs and Practices among Santals),* Manohar, (New Delhi, 1979), pp. 71-114.
8. Though formal theorization of the faith has not evolved, an implied scheme of doctrines may be discerned.
9. R.D. Munda expresses more or less similar view when he clusters *adivasi* faiths under *Adi-Dharm.* R.D. Munda, *Adi-Dharam,* Sarini and Birsa, Sarini Occasional Papers, No. 3 (Bhubaneswar, 2000), p. 44.
10. Past tense is used in this section to locate the faiths in time, though many of the beliefs and practices are relevant even today.
11. Lt. S.R. Tickell, 'Memoir on the Ho desum' (improperly called Kolehan)', *Journal of Asiatic Society of Bengal,* Vol. XI, part II, 1840, pp. 797-99; S.C. Roy, *The Oraons of Chotanagpur,* Ranchi, 1984, pp. 251-272; J. Hoffmann, *Encyclopaedia Mundarica,* Vol. 13, Gyan Publishing House, (New Delhi, Reprint 1998), pp. 3981-88; D.N. Majumdar, *A Tribe in Transition,* pp. 30,135; P.O. Bodding (Tr.), *Traditions and Institutions of the Santals/Horkoren Mare Hapramko Raek Katha,* Bahumukhi Prakashan, (New Delhi, Indian Reprint, 1994), pp. 3-22; J. Troisi, *Tribal Religion,* pp. 28-30; Van Exem, *The Religious System,* pp. 24-60; P.C. Hembrom, *Sari-Sarna* (*Santhal Religion*), Mittal Publications, (Delhi, 1988), pp. 6-12.
12. Tickell, 'Memoir', p. 797; Hoffman, *Encyclopaedia,* pp. 3973, 3976, 3978.
13. Roy, *Oraon Religion,* p. 14.
14. For details please see P. Sen, 'Understanding Tribal Cosmology and the Creation Myths of the Adivasis of Jharkhand', S. Gopal (ed), *Colonial India A Centenary Tribute to Professor K.K. Datta,* Research Publication Series-4, Veer Kunwar Singh University, Arrah, 2006
15. Bodding, *Traditions,* pp. 8-9.
16. Dalton, *Tribal History,* p. 256; Roy, *Oraon Religion,* pp. 15-16.
17. Troisi, *Tribal Religion,* pp. 238-74.
18. Birsa Munda (1874-1901) was originally a Christian by faith. But he lost faith in Christianity. He was influenced by his teacher Anand Panre and a monk who initiated him into Vaisnavism. Birsa

then claimed that he had the vision of *Singbonga* in his dream who had asked him to revive old Munda religion. Soon he started preaching his ideas among Mundas. He came to be known to his people as the *Dharti Aba* or the Father of the Earth or *Bhagwan*. This construction has drawn on: Roy, *The Mundas,* pp. 188-89; Singh, *Birsa Munda,* pp. 45-55; Sinha, *Life and Times,* pp. 72-77.

19. Kherwar is the original name used for Santals. They believed that during their halcyon days of the past they enjoyed an independent life without any material suffering. The aim of the Kherwar movement was to restore that past. But they believed that that past could be revived only when the impurities in their socio-religious system were removed. Leaders of this movement were Bhagirathi Majhi of Tardiha village in Godda subdivision of Santal Parganas and Dubia Gosain, a Hindu ascetic belonging to Jagesai of Hazaribag district in Chotanagpur. The movement was messianic as both the leaders proclaimed that God had sent them to redress the sufferings of Santals. This movement has been constructed on the basis of MacDougal, *Land or Religion,* pp, 72-88; Sinha, *Conflict and Tension,* pp. 200-222; S. Fuchs, *Rebellious Prophets,* p. 53; J. Troisi, *Tribal Religion,* pp. 71-114.
20. Roy, *Oraon Religion and Customs,* pp. 246-93, Sinha, *Conflict and Tension,* pp. 257-77, *Ekka, Tribal Movements,* pp. 221-45.
21. Areeparampil, 'Socio-Cultural and Religious Movements', pp. 397-98; A.D. Tuckey, *Final Report on the Resettlement of the Kolhan Government Estate in the District of Singhbhum 1913–1918* (Patna: Superintendent, Government Printing, Bihar and Orissa, (1920), p. 128.
22. Areeparampil, 'Socio-Cultural and Religious Movements', pp. 398-403; Singh, *Birsa Munda,* pp. 284-296.
23. MacDougal, *Land or Religion,* p. 74; Singh, *Birsa Munda,* pp. 53-55.
24. Singh, *Birsa Munda,* p. 157.
25. However, this induction again may be credited to the Christian as well as Vaisnava influences.
26. It may be interesting to note in this connection that propitiation of the pantheon is discarded but the existence of the spirits is not denied.
27. J. Troisi, 'Social Movements among the Santals', *Social Action,* Vol. 20, July-September, 1976, p. 265.
28. Sinha, *Life and Times,* p. 75; Singh, Birsa Munda, pp. 156-157.
29. Troisi, *Social Movements,* p. 265.
30. Munda, *Adi-Dharam,* p. 45.
31. They sought to develop their own scripts (*Ol Chiki* by Santals and *Waran Kshiti* by Hos), language and literature. This has received a spurt after the recent constitutional recognition granted to Santali

language. But one may discern in this the strengthening of inter-tribe solidarities around tribe-specific languages.

32. M. Areeparampil, *Struggle for Swaraj,* Tribal Research and Training Centre, Lupungutu, (Chaibasa, 2002), Chapter 9.
33. Areeparampil, *Socio-Cultural and Religious Movements,* p. 398; P.C. Hembram, 'Return to the Sacred Grove', in K.S. Singh (ed.), *Tribal Movement in India,* Vol. II, Manohar, (Delhi, 1983), pp. 87-91.
34. Munda, *Adi-Dharam,* pp. 4, 6.
35. P. Sen and A.K. Sen, 'Religion as Identity', pp. 247-258.

# 9

# Industries, Mines and Dispossession of Indigenous Peoples

## *The Case of Chotanagpur*

MATHEW AREEPARAMPIL

For a proper understanding of the problem of displacement of people due to the development of industries and mines we have to look at it from the wider perspective of the phenomenon of dispossession that result from such developmental activities. Displacement becomes a problem because of the dispossession that results from it. In this chapter, we shall consider the phenomenon of dispossession of the indigenous people of the Chotanagpur Plateau region in Middle India due to the gigantic industrial and mineral development programmes going on in that area.

### Chotanagpur Plateau : Its Main Characteristics

Chotanagpur forms the north-eastern portion of the Peninsular Plateau of India. Although its margins extend into Madhya Pradesh, Orissa and West Bengal, the bulk of it (about 79,476 sq. km.) lies in Bihar. The present study is concerned with only that portion of the Plateau which lies in Bihar and also the southern margin which lies in the Sundergarh district of Orissa.

The Plateau region of Chotanagpur and its surrounding areas were known as Jharkhand in ancient times. The word Jharkhand has special significance for this region. It expresses the characteristics of this region, namely, it is a forest and hilly tract. This region has a specific identity, it being a cultural unity in itself. This unity and identity is gradually getting destroyed due to the splitting of the region between four States and due to its becoming a victim of political, economic and cultural colonialism. Lately, the word Jharkhand has come to signify the agonies and aspirations of the masses of people who reside here.

The main characteristic of this area at present is the tremendous turmoil especially among its indigenous people. This turmoil is found not only in the economic and political fields but also in the social, cultural and religious spheres. It is manifested in various forms of *andolans* or people's struggles or agitations such as : the forest *andolan* in Singhbhum against the planting of teak and the commercialization of forests., The *Dhan Kato Andolan* or the forcible harvesting of paddy in Dhanbad, Giridih and Lohardaga areas for getting back the rights over land illegally taken away from the *adivasis, aandolan* against the construction of big dams like Koel Karo, Subarnarekha and Kutku; *andolan* for creation of a separate Jharkhand State, etc. The basic factor behind all this turmoil is the phenomenon of continued and systematic dispossession of the indigenous people of this area, displacement due to development projects being one of the most important types of such dispossessions. Sometimes many of these *andolans* have precipitated State violence against the indigenous people of this area. For example, during the period 1978-85 Singhbhum district alone witnessed 18 police firings on *adivasis* in which many innocent people were killed.

## Rich Land with Poor People

The Chotanagpur Plateau is one of the richest areas in the whole country, rich in minerals with huge reserves of coal, iron ore, mica, bauxite, and china clay and has considerable reserves of copper, manganese, limestone, atomic minerals, etc. The distribution of these minerals is mostly localised. Coal is found in the Gondwana rocks of the Damodar basin. Iron ore is associated with the iron-ore series of Dharwars confined to the Kolhan Upland. This region produces 48 per cent of the country's coal, 48 per cent of bauxite, 45 per cent of mica, 100 per cent of kyanite and 90 per cent of apatite. Revenue receipts from minerals of the region are increasing every year: from Rs. 41.4 crore to 114.3 crore in 1982-83. Besides, the region is rich in forests. Chotanagpur has 79 per cent of Bihar's forests area, with Singhbhum having Asia's richest Sal forests.

The natural wealth of this area contrasts vividly with the desperate poverty of the people who inhabit it. This region has been for ages the homeland of aboriginal races such as the Santals, Mundas, Oraons, Hos, Gonds, Kharias, Bhuiyas, Bhumij, Birhors, Dom, Turi, Sadans, Kamar, Kumhars, Kurmis, Tamarias, etc. These indigenous people of the area are also known as *adivasis* which literally means "original settlers", "earliest settlers", or "autochthones". They have a historical continuity with the pre-colonial societies that existed in this region. They have a *distinct* culture and identity which they are determined to preserve. Further, their identity and culture is rooted in their land. In contrast to the cultures of other people, it is this relationship which constitutes their very unique feature. As a result, they are more sensitive to protect their land from environmental deterioration than those who have or would take their land for so-called developmental projects. Their societies are community-based. Land is owned communally. Community life is cooperative and is based on sharing. Decisions are taken jointly through consensus. They thus consider their societies to be classless, egalitarian and close to nature. On the other hand, they see the societies around them as highly exploitative, stratified, centralised, individualistic, anti-nature and highly secular.

These indigenous groups comprising 85 to 90 per cent of the total population of Chotanagpur Plateau have been the worst hit by the large scale exploitation of the natural resources of the region through the development of industries, mines, and commercial exploitation of forests. The majority of them live in a state of semi-starvation throughout the year. The remaining 10 to 15 per cent of the population of the area are immigrants who have come here to amass wealth for themselves. The history of the indigenous people of the Chotanagpur Plateau is one of struggles against these alien exploiters whom they contemptuously call *dikus.* These *dikus* have gradually reduced them to a non-dominant position.

**Development of Chotanagpur Plateau**

Very few areas of the country are developing as fast as the Chotanagpur Plateau region. Industrialization began with the establishment of the first coal mining industry in Raniganj in the year 1775. In the year 1943, the first joint stock company M/s Bengal Coal Company was formed. After this chain of collieries were established on the left bank of the Damodar river. The famous Jharia coalfield in Dhanbad district is the richest treasure-house of India's metallurgical coal. The working of Jharia, Bokaro and Karanpura coalfields started in 1856. The opening of coal mining in Dhanbad area during the second half of the nineteenth century and the establishment of the Tata Iron & Steel Company in Jamshedpur in Singhbhum district in 1907 marked the beginning of the large scale exploitation of mineral and other industrial resources in this area.

The old pre-Cambrian rocks of Singhbhum-Orissa border known as Iron Ore series and Kolhan series constitute the chief iron belt of India. It is one of the richest iron belts in the world. The Department of Geology has recently reassessed the reserve of iron ore in this part, as of the order of 3,758 million tonnes with 60 per cent ferrous content. Fua, Jamda, Noamundi, Kiriburu, Chiria are the chief mines of the area, supplying iron ore to the steel plants at Jamshedpur, Rourkela, Bokaro, Durgapur and Bhilai. High grade iron ore are also exported. Between 1976 and 1980, the iron ore production from this area was of the order of 25 million tonnes.

Copper is another very important mineral which occurs in a 129 km. long belt from Duarpuram to Bahargora through Kharsawan, Seraikela and Dhalbhum. Total reserves of this area are about 153 million tonnes with 2.5 per cent copper content, mining centres. Copper is smelted by the Indian

Copper Corporation Ltd, which produces copper sheets, brass sheets etc. Between 1976 and 1980 the value of rupees of copper ore produced in the district was of the order of Rs 70.8 crore (Singh, 1981).

Mica is another important nmineral in which the Chotanagpur Plateau leads not only the Indian States but all the countries of the world. The mica belt covering about 3,800 sq. km. lies in the heart of this region. The belt supplies over 71 per cent of the world's high quality sheet mica. Limestone is the chief material of cement. It is quarried mainly in Singhbhum, Hazaribagh and Ranchi districts. Kyanite is an important refractory mineral used in the iron and steel industry. The world's largest deposits of high grade kyanite occur at Lapsa Buru in Singhbhum. This mineral also enables the country to earn a good deal of foreign exchange. During 1977-1980, the district produced about 1 lakh tonnes of high grade kyanite. Bauxite is growing in importance as the raw material of aluminium industry. In Chotanagpur bauxite quarries are located in and around the Pat region in north-west Ranchi district within a radius of 9-30 km. from Lohardaga.

Besides the above china clay mining is developed mainly in the Hat Gahmaria area of Singhbhum and also in Palamau, Ranchi and Santal Parganas. Fire clay mining and its associated industries have developed in the Damodar basin in Jharia and Raniganj coal fields. Mining of manganese, apatite, chromite, quartz and silica, stearite and asbestos have developed on a large scale in various parts of Singhbhum district. Dolomite is mined in Palamau and Singhbhum. The Uranium Corporation of India Ltd, a public sector undertaking, has established an atomic plant at Jadugora in Singhbhum and has started mining of uranium at Bhatian, Narwapahar, Turamdih and other areas in Singhbhum.

The industrial landscape of Chotanagpur Plateau has undergone considerable change during recent years mainly around Jamshedpur, Rourkela, Ranchi, and Bokaro and in the coal mining areas of Dhanbad and Ramgarh. The large scale industries of these centres are based mostly on the vast metalic and non-metallic mineral resources available in the area. Jamshedpur with Tata Iron & Steel Company is the most important industrial centre of the region. There are about forty large and medium industries in Singhbhum alone employing more than forty thousand labourers. The number of small scale industries in this district is about 200. The establishment of huge iron and steel plants at Rourkela in Sundergarh district and at Bokaro in Dhanbad district has turned also those two areas into major industrial centres of the region. Ranchi has become another important industrial centre with the location of the Heavy Engineering Corporation at Hatia. All these centres have attracted a large number of other industries in their suburbs and adjoining areas. The non-metallic mineral industries are mainly situated in the Damodar basin centred on Dhanbad and Ramgarh.

The important non-metallic mineral industries include cement factories at Japla (Palamau), Jhinkpani (Singhbhum), fertiliser factories at Sindri and Rourkela, refractory works at Dhanbad and Ramgarh, glass factories at Kandra (Singhbhum) and Bhurkunda (Hazaribagh), mica industries at Jhumri-Telaiya and Giridih and coal washeries and coke oven plants in Hazaribagh and Dhanbad districts. Besides, a large number of medium and small industrial hubs of forest and agriculture-based industries, small engineering and manufacturing industries, chemical industries, etc. have developed at other centres such as Chaibasa, Chakradharpur, Daltonganj, Gumla, Muri, Latehar, Chatra, Ghatsila, Khunti, Chandil, etc. Large thermal power generating plants have been built at Bokaro, Patratu, Chandrapra and Sindri in the Damodar basin and at Jamshedpur in Singhbhum. Hydro-electricity is generated by the Damodar Valley Corporation at its plants at Telaiya, Konar, Pachet and Maithon. These plants supply power for industries in the Chotanagpur Plateau and adjoining areas.

Till the beginning of the present century the Chotanagpur Plateau area had very few urban centres. The few which existed were mainly administrative towns. With the intensification of mining and manufacturing activities, especially after independence this region has registered a phenomenal growth in urbanisation. From less than two per cent at the beginning of the century and 11.5 per cent in 1961, the urban population has grown to 20.8 per cent in 1981. The number of towns increased from 8 in 1872 to 65 in 1961. This percentage is higher than that in the plains of Bihar. This rapid urban growth is due mainly to the rapid industrialisation and mineral exploitation programme going on in the region. Thus the urban centres are mainly concentrated in the Damodar and Subarnarekha basins which are the two main mining and manufacturing zones of the region.

The industrial revolution that is taking place in the Chotanagpur Plateau as a result of the exploitation of its vast mineral resources, the establishment of industries and hydro-electric projects on a large scale, and the phenomenal growth in urbanisation are in fact causing an explosion of various sorts in the area. One can call it an explosion because of the totally unparalleled scope and the catastrophic nature of the changes that it is bringing about in this region. It is causing an unprecendented assault on the relatively stable and self-sufficient indigenous people and their land and other resources. We shall now examine the impact of these changes on the indigenous people of this region.

## Indigenous People of Chotanagpur Plateau : Victims of Development

The basic phenomenon that characterises the situation of indigenous people of Chotanagpur Plateau is that of dispossession. They are systematically and methodically being dispossessed of the ownership of their means of production, of the products of their labour and of the very means of human existence. They are dispossessed of their political autonomy and their communities are being broken up in the name of 'development' and 'national interest'. They are dispossessed of their cultures, their values, and their very identity through well planned policies, such as those of integration and assimilation, of bringing them to the so-called 'national mainstream'. This phenomenon of dispossession takes place both directly through deprivation of their land, for example, and indirectly thorough denial of the benefits of development, of their rights, etc.

## Process of Dispossession of Indigenous People

The phenomenon of dispossession of indigenous people in the Chotanagpur Plateau started when colonisation in its march for resources began penetrating their areas. It is true that external colonialism in India ended with the departure of the British. But the process of colonial exploitation of these people did not stop with independence. In the name of 'development' for 'national interest', a new type of internal colonialism is being unleashed on them by the ruling classes of the country. Let us now see how this dispossession is taking place in the various spheres—economic, social, political and cultural.

## Dispossession in the Economic Sphere

### *(a) Land Alienation and Displacement*

As we have seen earlier, the indigenous people have a special relationship with the land they hold. To them land is not simply a factor of production as for other people, but sources of spirituality as well. The traditional land base holds important symbolic and emotional meaning for them as the repository for ancestral remains, clan origin sites and other sacred features important to their religious system. Regarding ownership of land the indigenous people have different concepts, often incomprehensible to outsideres. In the first place, ownership of land is vested in the community. No Individual has the right to permanently alienate the land from the community. The tribe is the trustee of the land it occupies. The community or tribe includes not only the living members but also the ancestors and future generations. That is why for the indigenous people land and blood is homologous. Their society, culture, religion, identity and their very existence are intimately linked to the land they hold. As an aboriginal leader from Australia said :

> My land is my backbone . . . I only stand straight, happy, proud and not ashamed[1] about my colour because I still have land. I can dance, paint, create and sing as my ancestors did before me . . . My land is my foundation. I stand, live and perform as long as I have something firm and hard to stand on. Without land . . . we will be the lowest people in the world, because you have broken down our backbone, took away my arts, history and foundation. You have left us with nothing (quoted in Roberts 1978 : 5-6).

To separate the indigenous people from their lands is tantamount to tearing them apart from their life-giving source. But colonial exploitation of their territories has meant precisely that for many of the indigenous people of Chotanagpur Plateau. A large number of them have been illegally dispossessed of their lands. Many have been forced to leave their homes to work in the brick kilns and stone quarries of North Bihar, West Bengal, U.P., Punjab and other places as contract and even bonded labourers. The gaping black holes of abandoned pits scattered all over Chotanagpur Plateau, left after the plundering of its mineral wealth, symbolise prophetically the ultimate fate of the indigenous people of the region.

### *(b) Extent of Land Alienation and Displacement*

Although the exact extent of land alienation and displacement due to industrial and mineral development in the Chotanagpur Plateau area is difficult to ascertain, we shall try here to get a rough picture of the situation by examining the extent of dispalcement caused by some of the major projects of the area.

#### *(i) Mining Industry*

One of the major causes of land alienation and displacement in the area is the mining industry, particularly coal. In the past coal mining was done by private firms. Vast tracts in the coal bearing area of Damodar Valley have been acquired by those firms often by fraud and turned into wastelands by haphazard mining. After the nationalisation of the coal industry (coking coal in 1971 and non-coking coal in 1973) the coal mining in this region is entrusted to Coal India Ltd. (CCL) and its subsidiary companies mentioned below :

1. Bharat Coking Coal Ltd. (BCCL) has in its charge 390 nationalised mines and Sudamdih and Moonidih mines which were earlier owned by NCDC.
2. Eastern Coalfields Ltd. (ECL) covers the Raniganj coalfields in West Bengal and Mugma Rajmahal coalfields in Bihar.
3. Central Coalfields Ltd. (CCL) covers the Bokaro, Ramgarh, Giridih and North and South Karanpura coalfields in Bihar, the Talcher coalfields in Orissa and Singrauli coalfields of M.P. and U.P. The company owns 57 coal mines, 4 coal washeries and a by-product coke plant.

These coal companies' area at present acquiring extensive land areas and displacing a large number of families. According to an estimate, between 1981 and 1985, the Central Coalfields Ltd. has acquired 1,300 acres of land. Similarly Eastern Coalfields Ltd. has acquired about 30,000 acres during the Sixth Plan period. More than 32,750 families have been displaced. But Coal India could offer jobs only to 11,901 displaced people (see Table 9.1).

**Table 9.1:** Number of Families Displaced and Number of Jobs provided by CCL

| *Sl. No.* | *Company* | *No. of Families Displaced* | *No. of Jobs provided to One Member of the Family* |
|---|---|---|---|
| 1. | Eastern Coalfields Ltd. | 14,750 | 4,915 |
| 2. | Central Coalfields Ltd. | 7,928 | 3,984 |
| 3. | Western Coalfields Ltd | 6,232 | 2,250 |
| 4. | Bharat Coking Coal Ltd. | 3,841 | 752 |
| | Total | 32,751 | 11,901 |

*Source*: Govt. of India 1985.

Even after nationalisation much illegal mining by private contractors is going on all over the Chotanagpur Plateau. Vast areas of agricultural land belonging to indigenous people are being laid waste because of haphazard mining. Further, excessive underground mining of coal is causing subsidence of land in many areas as a result of which such lands have been rendered unsafe for habitation, agriculture and grazing.

After the Damodar Valley the next important area of mining activity in the region is the district of Singhbhum. According to the Director of Mines and Mine Leases published by the Indian Bureau of Mines, Nagpur, there were about 300 mines operating in Sinbhghum in the year 1974 and more than 1,51,000 acres of land were leased out, owned mostly by private agencies. However, the total land area affected by mining is many times greater than the simple lease area. Lot of land is illegally mined by private contractors. Besides, land is also converted to such purposes as roads, township for miners, infrastructure for administrative purposes, stockyard for preliminary processing operations, etc. Further, disposal of mining debris creates pollution and makes agricultural fields infertile which forces the people to abandon or alienate their lands and move out to other areas.

*(ii) Industrial Concerns*

Industrial concerns have added to this alienation. The pioneering industrial concern of the region. Tata Iron & Steel Company (established in 1907 at Sakchi now known as Jamshedpur), initially acquired 3,564 acres of land comprising the villages of Sakchi, Nutandi, Susnidih and the northern part of Jugsalai at the cost of Rs.46,332. Regarding the original inhabitants of these villages Dr. Maya Dutta (1977:12) says : "Some old residents of Jamshedpur seem to be unanimous about the virtual disappearance of the original tribal inhabitant."

The construction of the first steel plant of independent India began in 1956 at Rourkela, in the Sundergarh district of Orissa. At the time of its selection for the steel plant, Rourkela was a remote tribal area of 32 villages with 2,465 families of which 70 per cent were tribals. All these families were displaced. However, at present only 1,200 families are to be found rehabilitated in the two settlement colonies at Jalda and Jhirpani. According to a letter of D.N. Tiwari, Director, Ministry of Home Affairs, for the construction of the Rourkela plant, mines, and the Mandira Dam, 32,567,71 acres of land were acquired resulting in the displacement of 4,251 families. The families displaced by the Mandira Dam were resettled in camps at Laing, Khandapahar, Lachchara, Mandalia, Jaidega and Banikibhal (Government of India, 1985). According to the Dhebar Commission Report, 1,231 Scheduled Tribes families were displaced for the Rourkela Steel Project from 8,158 acres of land and only 843 of them were settled on land; for the Mandira Dam 817 ST families were displaced from 4,225 acres and only 447 of them were settled on a total area of 1,696 acres. (Dhebar 1961:115). As of June 1984, Rourkela had provided employment, under the T.N. Singh formula to 4,607 displaced persons including tribals (Govt. of India 1985). The Rourkela plant has a proposal to acquire 320 acres of land for dolomite mining at Gattitanagar (Purnapani) (*ibid.*).

The Heavy Engineering Corporation Ltd, established at Hatia near Ranchi in 1958, acquired 9,200 acres of land for the purpose of constructing factories, township, railways, dam, etc. This land was acquired from 25 villages, out of which 12 villages were acquired fully and the rest partly. As a result, 2,198 families or a total population of 12,990 were displaced. These families belonged to Oraon and Munda tribes and some Hindu castes. Only some of these families were rehabilitated.

Bokaro Steel Ltd. is the largest steel plant in India. Its construction started in 1967; 46 villages were acquired for the construction of the plant and the township. 30,984.22 acres of land were acquired displacing 12,487 families, 2,707 of them tribal. Bokaro has given employment to 14,000 displaced persons which include 2,776 tribals (*ibid.*).

Nirmal Sen Gupta (1979:75) has well described the plight to which the Bauris, an indigenous community of the area, has been reduced because of the development of the Bokaro Steel Plant.

On the eve of the construction of the steel plant, 62 per cent of the Bauris of Chas-Telidih area and cent per cent rural Bauris had their own house sites though only 24 per cent of the former and 88 per cent of the latter had cultivable land.

This was the situation up to 1965. After that everything changed suddenly. Large areas were acquired for the setting up of the steel plant and the new township as a result of which many peasant and village households were evicted. Further, because of the increase in the value of land in the surrounding areas, land transfer became very frequent. By 1978, the one time cultivators of the area now acquired by the steel plant, were completely dispossessed. Among those in the Chas-Telidih areas, less than five per cent were engaged in agriculture, and in rural areas almost every household had sold at least a part of its cultivable land (*ibid.*, 109).

The case of the Bauri Community clearly shows how the indigenous people are being dispossessed and turned into destitutes due to the gigantic industrialisation programme going on in the Chotanagpur Plateau. As Sachidananda says in his foreword to the book of Sen Gupta, the big industrial complexes in the tribal and backward areas are only peaks of excellence for the nation but that for many local communities they have spelled disaster.

*(iii) Urbanisation*

The rapid expansion of industries and mines in the Chotanagpur Plateau was followed by a phenomenal growth in urbanisation and large scale influx of outsiders to the area. This, in turn, has resulted in increased land alienation and displacement of indigenous people. The displacement caused by the expansion of the industrial-urban sector further resulted in many cases in the migration of indigenous people to outside regions in search of livelihood. The immigrant outsiders have legally or by fraud displaced the indigenous people from their habitat. The extent of the influx of these outsiders to the area can be seen from the fall in the proportion of STs and SCs to the total population of the area : in Singhbhum the proportion of STs and SCs to the total population fell from 58.54 per cent in 1931 to 48.87 per cent in 1981; the proportion of ST alone fell from 54.08 per cent in 1931 to 44.08 per cent in 1981. In 1971, there were 3,10,253 persons living in Singhbhum who were born outside the Chotanagpur region and they constituted 12.73 per cent of the total population of the district. The situation is similar in other parts of the Chotanagpur Plateau. Districts like Dhanbad, Ranchi, and Santal Parganas have also had very great increase in the number of immigrants. During 1971-1981 alone the proportion of STs to the total population in the whole Chotanagpur and Santal Parganas fell from 32.1 per cent to 30.26 per cent. This clearly shows the rapid increase in the influx of outsiders to the areas.

**Mechanism of Land Alienation and Displacement**

The most important way in which the indigenous people are dispossessed of their land is the so-called 'legal' method of acquiring land for 'public purpose'. The Chotanagpur Tenancy Act (CNT) passed in 1908 prohibited the alienation of tribal land to non-tribals. This law was an impediment to the new industrial-urban development. As a result, the CNT Act was amended in 1947 by the addition of Section 49, so that tribal land could be acquired for the purposes of urbanisation and industrialisation and for developmental projects.

The random financial compensation and the "Rehabilitation Schemes" for the tribal lands expropriated by under Section 49 of the CNT Act are mostly inadequate and most often this section is widely misused by vested interests. In spite of the various restrictions laid down in the CNT Act. Large areas of tribal lands have been alienated by these vested interests. The State and its administration (Controlled mostly by people from North Bihar), instead of protecting the poor tribals have become a major party to this alienation. Further, the CNT Act is being subverted by employing the wide-ranging Land Alienation Act on the basis of which tribal lands can be acquired for 'public purpose'. The term 'public purpose' in this Act is so broad that it can be used to sanction land for practically any purpose.

One of the main ways of circumventing the CNT Act is to sanction a new project like an irrigation scheme, experimental farm, industry, etc. and acquire a larger area than required for 'public purpose'. The excess land is then leased out to the friends of the officials and politicians. At times the project itself collapses within a few years. But the land is not returned to the original owners, but alienated for other purposes. The best example is the Roro Irrigation Scheme near Chaibasa. Through a gazette notification tribal land was acquired for the purpose of constructing an irrigation canal. Under this pretext the Irrigation Department, Government of Bihar acquired large areas of tribal land on both sides of the canal. These lands are now being used for constructing quarters for non-tribals. Big walls have come up on both sides of the canal as a result of which it is impossible for the tribals to take water from the canal irrigation and other purposes.

In order to prevent such misuse the term 'public purpose' should be properly defined and restrictions should be placed on excessive acquisition of land. Land should be acquired or purchased from the indigenous people only when and to the extent strictly necessary. So far as possible, only barren or unirrigated land should be acquired. Further, if the acquired land is not used for the specific purpose for which it was acquired, it should be returned to the original owners.

Moreover, it seems that there is a well-planned conspiracy by certain vested interests (e.g. those influenced by religious fanaticism like RSS) in the administration to systematically displace and dispossess people belonging to certain communities (e.g. Tribals, Christians, Muslims, etc.) by purposely locating certain projects in areas where such communities are predominant, even when other areas far more suitable for the same purpose.

The displacement of indigenous people can also occur through indirect pressure on their life by the establishment of industries, mines, towns, etc. One such factor which forces them to move out of their habitats is pollution of air and water in the surrounding areas. For example, the cement dust from the ACC cement factory at Jhinkpani in Singhbhum is polluting the air and making vast areas of agricultural land practically useless. The red oxide from the slag dams at Noamundi iron ore mines has destroyed vast areas of paddy fields during the rainy season in several villages around them. Besides, the *adivasis* have an aversion towards the *dikus* and move out of their areas because of the conflict of cultures when the *dikus* become a majority there. The increasing criminalisation of society in the industrial-urban sector due to robbery, goondaism, prostitution, communal riots, etc. is another reason for the simple indigenous people to opt out of such areas. This negative situation of urban pressure is accompanied by rising price offers by speculators for building land as incitement for selling their lands. This push and pull effect has indirectly forced the indigenous people to move out of their hearths and homes.

In the race for acquiring land, the speculators, if they fail to find the way of voluntary selling, use illegal and even strong arm methods to evict the original owners. In the beginning the indigenous owners are implicated in false litigation plotted ingeniously with the help of corrupt officials. In many cases the poor owners have to sell their land to fight these cases. If this method fails, then naked force too is resorted to. The case of Fulmani Bourin mentioned in Nirmal Sen Gupta's book is a typical example of the poor unable to take possession of their land even after winning in the court, because of the strong arm tactics adopted by the mafia.

In the Kolhan area of Singhbhum there are more than 250 mines most of which are privately operated by contractors coming from outside Chotanagpur. In many cases they illegally take away the lands for mining purposes after driving out the tribal *raiyats* from their agricultural lands. They destroy the tribals' worshipping and burial places, sometimes give them a nominal sum as compensation and start mining, often with the help of the local police and *goondas*. The original owners are made to work as *rejas* and *coolies* in their own lands at starvation wages. The irony of the situation is that the *raiyats* are still paying the *malguzari* (tax) on these lands.

In a question in the Lok Sabha, A.K. Roy, M.P. had alleged that the Tata Company had illegally alienated *adivasi raiyati* land at Noamundi for establishing a pelletising plant there and that the ACC Company at Jhinkpani had illegally take *adivasi* land for its mining activities. The Land Revenue Deputy Collector, Sadar, Chaibasa made a detailed inquiry regarding these allegations and submitted a report to the SDO, Sadar, Chaibasa on August 4, 1983. His report showed that the allegations were true. Regarding the Noamundi case the report stated :

> It is clear from the evidence of the facts of the records that some of the *raiyats* were made to sign or put the thumb impression in the names of dead persons by the company. In some *khewats* in the name of dead persons and other persons have put false signatures. In some, in the place of minors, some others have put the signature. Those people who have their names in the *khewat* as the ones who have sold their lands are the one who are filing cases against the Company, for the restoration of their lands. This shows that the land has been illegally occupied. It seems that through deceit the *raiyats* have been made to sign on the papers and the officers were tricked to get the permission for transfer of the land. In the way the *adivasi* lands have been illegally alienated by the Company (Translated from Hindi).

The report showed that also the ACC Company at Jhinkpani and some private mining contractors had illegally taken away *adivasi* land for mining purposes. In this way the indigenous people are being dispossessed of their lands illegally in parts of Chotanagpur by the vested interests.

**Compensation**

As regards compensation, employment and rehabilitation the policy adopted by the Government is very unjust and inequitable. The displaced people are being paid only for their land house. Further, compensation is paid mainly in monetary terms. For the indigenous people monetary compensation has very little value. First of all, it is very meagre for their rehabilitation as they will not be able to buy land at other places at high rates. Secondly, since the only skill they have is farming, they will not be able to put the money to commercial use. They will either eat it up or will be swindled. Further, cash compensation has also created mistrust and division in many families who were otherwise living peacefully. Some clever and stronger members of the families have fraudulently deprived the weaker ones like widows, old women, etc. of their rightful compensation and misappropriated it for themselves, often in connivance with corrupt officials.

There are also cases of non-payment of compensation and non-provision of resettlement facilities to the displaced even after many years. Recently a press report said that people of several villages (Purhara, Bacchai, Hazari, Bedgi, Kolli, Ovara, and Sewai) in Bathi block in Hazaribagh district which were submerged by the Tilaiya Dam of DVC have not yet received any compensation or any provision for resettlement (*Ranchi Express*, March 15, 1988).

**Who Gets the Benefits?**

A look at the number of SC and ST workers engaged in different industrial categories in Chotanagpur and Santal Parganas in 1981 shows that though they constitute 42 per cent of the total population and 48 per cent of the main workers, their share in benefits arising out of the development of the region is minimal. Only 26.75 per cent of the main workers employed in different industries in the region belonged to SCs and STs. Further, nearly 60 per cent of the marginal workers, i.e. those who worked for less than six months during the year belonged to SC and ST. In fact 18.4 per cent of the total SC and ST workers belong to this category. Similarly, although 20.3 per cent of the total population of the district lives in the urban areas, only 19 per cent of the urban population belongs to SC and ST. Dhanbad, one of the most urbanised districts in India, has 50.62 per cent of its total population living in the urban areas. However, only 17.87 per cent of the urban population of

Dhanbad belongs to SC and ST. Jamshedpur town situated in the heart of the tribal area, has only 4.96 per cent of its population belonging to ST. Most of them live in the slum areas and work as *rejas* and *coolies*. The immigrants who account for about 10 to 15 per cent of the total population of the Chotanagpur Plateau have appropriated most of the employment opportunities opened up in the region by the large scale development activities of the last few decades.

The urban centres are enclaves of prosperity in this backward region. The entepreneurs in these urban centres are mostly outsiders who invest their profits in other parts of India. The best example of this is the coal mining towns of Dhanbad. The economic linkages between the urban belt and its immediate hinterland are conspicuous by their absence. The industrial and rural sectors are separated from each other by a sharp dividing line which has been accentuated and not eliminated by economic development. What we have in the Chotanagpur Plateau is urban growth and rural stagnation or prosperity of the few at the expense of the majority.

## Social, Political and Cultural Dispossession

The dispossession of the indigenous people of the Chotanagpur Plateau due to various development projects is taking place not only in the economic but also in the social, political and cultural spheres. As a result of the new forces that are being introduced among them and also due to the rapid change that is taking place in their economic condition, also the social structures of the indigenous societies are breaking down. Their family life is getting disrupted. They are losing their traditional social controls and social tension is increasing among them. They are becoming more and more vulnerable to disease and emotional disorders. Many indicators of social anomie such as alcoholism, crime, suicide, prostitution, delinquency and despair have gone up suddenly? Further, these people confronted with development and modernisations are often experiencing a loss of self-esteem. They are feeling the deprivation of their sense of personal worth and a devaluation of their social identity. This feeling is further aggravated by the negative attitude and approach of the dominant society towards their culture. As a result of this continual and systematic process of dispossession and disruption of their society, the indigenous people of this area are gradually being reduced to a sub-human level of existence.

In the political sphere the dispossession of indigenous people takes place through the process of their political integration in the so-called national polity as a result of which their traditional political institutions are destroyed. They are incorporated into the State and they have to conform to and become integrated with the political institution of the dominant society. In order to achieve their complete political integration, Political auhthorities belonging to the dominant society are appointed over them. As a result of all this they have become politically powerless and are marginalised and exploited by the dominant society.

Because of all the above factors the cultures of these societies are also gradually disintegrating. This process of disintegration of their traditional cultures is further accelerated by deliberate programmes of 'integration' and 'assimilation' followed by the State to bring the indigenous people to the so called national mainstream. They have been dispossessed of their cultural autonomy and their very identity has been lost. Every area of their life from language to marriage customs and religion has come under attack. Language is the main comenting factor that expresses the identity of a given community. There is a non-declared polity to suppress the language of the indigenous people and to impose on them the dominant language of the area. According to a well known Indian sociologist, the tribal languages are "merely corruptions of good speech and unworthy of survival" (Ghurye 1963, 187). The suppression of the language of the indigenous people is one of the most effective ways of keeping them oppressed so that they can be easily exploited.

A result of the dispossession of indigenous people that is taking place in the economic, political and social spheres is a gradual collapse of their religious ethos which is closely linked to their socio-agrarian system. The new forces of change that have come up are beyond the framework of their traditional religious system. The inevitable frustration resulting from this continual deprivation finds expression in the formation of new forms of religious, revitalisation has been able to collect information on more than 15 new religious movements among the Ho tribals of Singhbhum along. These movements are signs of the turmoil that is taking place in their society.

## Consequence of Dispossession

What we have in the Chotanagpur Plateau is organised alienation of the region's riches in favour of a few powerful elements and the consequent starvation of the majority. The rich exploiters not only rob the indigenous people of their wealth but also treat them with contempt. They have no regard for the language and culture of the indigenous people. They create division and tension among these simple peace loving people through their machinations. They create communal hatred between tribals and non-tribals of the area. The vested interests and communal forces have joined hands to break the solidarity of the indigenous people and to demoralise them. Towns like Jamshedpur, Hazaribagh, Ranchi, Chaibasa and Bokaro have become areas of communal tension by converting this region into a fertile ground of communalism and these forces are aiming to break the solidarity of the indigenous people in order to keep them in eternal bondage so that they can carry on their looting of the area unopposed.

The result of this organised alienation of the riches of the area is utter misery. Virtually nothing has been done for the welfare of the villagers. It is said that the Chotanagpur Plateau provides 72 per cent of the entire revenue of the State of Bihar, but plan allocation for this area is barely 20 per cent and most of that dries up in the pipeline. The Chotanagpur and Santal Parganas area comprising half of Bihar State and only 2.5 per cent of the whole country produces 90 per cent and 7 per cent of the total electricity generated in Bihar and India respectively. But the proportion of villages electrified in this region is one of the lowest in the whole country.

Most villages are isolated and unapproachable due to lack of proper roads. Schools in many villages exist only on paper, and the salary of their teachers are divided among the corrupt officials of the education department. Medical facilities are all but non-existent. As a result, the indigenous people resort to the only facility available to them—the witch doctors. Agriculture is their sole means of livelihood. Due to frequent failure of rains, the income from this source is too minimal. Very few viable irrigation schemes exist in this region. A report in the New *Republic,* Ranchi (December 13, 1986) showed that 400 irrigation schemes which were claimed by the Government to have been completed were in fact lying incomplete. As a result of all this, many indigenous people have mortgaged their lands to the rich villagers and a large number have lost them to the mining contractors and become paupers and *coolies* in the brick kilns.

Because of the systematic dispossession of the masses of people living in this region we have a situation of a few powerful and rich monopolising the resources and exploiting the poverty and powerlessness of the people. Thus although the Chotanagpur Plateau is developing at a very fast rate through the process of industrialisation and mining, its inhabitants are among the worst underdeveloped group in the whole country. Hence it is important to have a look at the dynamics of this underdevelopment.

## Dynamics of Underdevelopment

### *(a) The Haves thrive on the Misery of the Have-nots*

On the eve of the 33rd anniversary of independence in 1980, the President of India said in a broadcast to the nation :

> The rising prices and increasing disparities, making the rich much richer and the poor still poorer, are widening the gulf between the few haves thriving on the miseries of the have-nots, and the deprived masses left with little hope of any better life in the foreseeable future (quoted in *Sunday,* Aug. 17, 1980).

According to Ranjit Sau, in this statement the President has correctly enunciated three basic facts regarding the present Indian situation. They eminently characterise the situation in the Chotanagpur Plateau.

1. The gulf between the few rich and the many poors is widening;
2. The haves thrive on the misery of the have-nots; and
3. There is little hope of any better life for the deprived masses in the foreseeable future.

The second proposition—the haves thrive on the misery of the have-nots—is one of the most paradoxical iron laws of the development process that is taking place in areas where indigenous people live. It needs further explanation.

### *(b) National Interest and Enslavement of Indigenous People*

We have seen that the Chotanagpur Plateau is one of the richest areas in the whole country, rich in minerals and forests. At the same time it is also the homeland of a large number of indigenous people who live in utter poverty. Further, in the name of *national interest* this area is witnessing a gigantic industrialisation process for the exploitation of its natural wealth. This ideology of *national interest* (which is nothing but the interest of the ruling capitalist class) is the guiding principle behind the process of development that is taking place in this area. In other words, in the name of *national interest* the Chotanagpur Plateau is witnessing not development but the rape of its people and of its natural wealth through a process of colonialist and capitalist exploitation. The brutality displayed on the land and the people of this area, by the process of industrialisation, by the plundering of its mineral wealth, and by the decimation of its forests which provided much of the livelihood for its people, has not only reduced the majority of its inhabitants to destitution but has also brought the area to the brink of an ecological disaster.

The large scale capitalist exploitation of the wealth of the Chotanagpur Plateau required a vast army of cheap casual labour. The indigenous people who are reduced to destitution are forced to accept this role. The capitalist development and exploitation has thus operated in a various circle for the indigenous people. On the one hand, it has rendered ever increasing numbers of the destitutes through eviction, destination of their source of livelihood, etc. and on the other, it has utilised their destitute condition to employ them for a specific role in this process namely, that of sweat labour of the proletariat. The process of development has done this in the name of *national interest.* Moreover, every attempt is made to keep them in such a situation because without them remaining in such a state, no 'development' is possible. Thus they typify the following liberalist view quoted by Thomas P. Nelle (1953, 80).

Without a large proportion of poverty there could be no riches, since riches are the offsprings of labour, while labour can result only from a state of poverty. Poverty, therefore, is a most necessary and indispensable ingredient in society, without which nations and communities could not exist in a state of civilisation.

Another liberalist wrote :

> Everyone but an idiot knows that the lower classes must be kept poor, or they will never be industrious *(ibid., 56).*

Thus poverty and the poor are absolutely essential for the very survival of the system which exists in our country.

## Proletarianisation of Indigenous People through Displacement and Rehabilitation Programmes

Let us now look at the process of proletarianisation and enslavement of indigenous people that occurs through the displacement and rehabilitation programmes adopted in various development projects. The first step in this process is the disassociation of the indigenous people from the ownership of their subsistent and self-sufficient economy is destroyed.

They are turned into 'free workers' independent from and deprived of the material means of their own reproduction. For their survival they have to depend solely on the sale of their labour power. This conversion of self-sufficient farmers into cheap wage labourers is the first precondition for the spread of capitalist relations of production.

The second step in this process is the creation of 'labour colonies' or forced settlements. This is achieved through the resettlement and rehabilitation programmes adopted by the government. The displaced people are settled in groups on government and other lands and each family is provided with a small plot of homestead land. This small plot of land is given so that the indigenous people can undertake subsistence production when they are not needed as wage labourers. This subsistence production helps to keep the labour force cheap since by cultivating the small plot of land the workers obtain part of their own consumption needs. In this way, a vast army of cheap labour force is 'conserved' and the permanent availability of its labour power assured.

The third step in the proletarianisation of indigenous people is their 'disciplining' and training. For the capitalist exploitation of the area it is necessary to create a particular class of worker out of the indigenous people. They have to be 'disciplined' and trained for the type of work (as *rejas* and *coolies*, for example), they have to perform, because the indigenous people in general are neither willing nor prepared to work as wage labourers. The rehabilitation programmes have various provisions for achieving this purpose.

In this way the indigenous people of the Chotanagpur Plateau are gradually being reduced to a proletariat by the large scale industrialization and mining programmes going on in this area. They are being systematically and methodically dispossessed of the ownership of their means of production, of the product of their labour and of the very means of human existence. This systematic dispossession is resulting in starvation, squalor, disease and deprivation. Regarding the enslavement and degradation of the indigenous people of India Nirad C. Chaudhuri wrote thus : "In an industrialised Indian the destruction of aboriginal's life is as inevitable as the submergence of the Egyptian temples caused by the dams of the Nile . . . . As thing are going there can be no grandeur in the primitive's end. It will not be even simple extinction, which is not the worst of human destinies. It is to be feared that the aboriginal's last act will be squalid, instead of being tragic. What will be seen with most regret will be, not his disappearance, but his enslavement and degradation (quoted in Haimendrof 1982, 312).

## Conclusion

In this chapter we have seen that the Chotanagpur Pleteau is an area very rich in minerals and forest. It is the homeland of a large number of indigenous people who live in harmonious relationship with their environment. Further, we saw that in the name of *"national interest"* this area is witnessing a gigantic industrialisation and development process for the exploitation of its natural and human resources. This capitalist from the development is leading to the large scale dispossession and proletarianisation of the indigenous people of this area. Can this process be reversed? The struggles and turmoil in the reason give some hope but the repression that follows leads one to despair.

## ACKNOWLEDGEMENT

This essay has been reprinted from W. Fernandes and E.G. Thukral (eds.), *Development, Displacement and Rehabilitation*, Indian Social Institute, New Delhi, 1989. We thank the Director, Tribal Research and Training Centre, Bara Guira, Chaibasa for kindly allowing us the permission to include this essay in this volume.

## REFERENCES

Dhebar, *U.N. Report of the Scheduled Areas and Scheduled Tribes Commission, Vol. I*, 1960-61 (New Delhi, Ministry of Home Affairs, Govt. of India, 1961).

Dutta, Manju, Jamshedpur: *The Growth of the City and its Regions* (Calcutta: The Asiatic Society, 1977).

Ghurye, G.S., *The Scheduled Tribes* (Bombey, Popular Prakashan, 1963).

Haimendorf, Curistoph Von Fuver, *Tribes of India: The Struggle of Survival* (Delhi, Oxford University Press, 1982).

Neil, Thomas,P., *The Rise and Decline of Liberalism* (Milmankee: Bruce Publishing Co., 1953).

*Report of the Committee on Rehabilitation of Displaced Tribals due to Development Projects* (New Delhi, Ministry of Home Affairs, 1985)

Roberts, Jaine, *From Massacre to Mining: The Colonisation of Aboriginal Australia* (London: CIMRA, 1978).

Sengupta, Nirmal, *Destitutes and Development: Study of Bauri Community in Bokaro Region* (New Delhi: Concept Publishing Co., 1979).

Singh, Rajendra Pratap, *Mineral Development Strategy: The Indian Nation (June 10, 1981).*

# 10

# Indigenous Movements for a Separate State—Jharkhand during the Twentieth Century

ASHA MISHRA

For ages Jharkhand has been the homeland of some of India's major *adivasi* communities such as the Gonds, Santhals, Oraons, Mundas, Khonds, Hos, Kharias, Bhumij, Birhors etc. Nearly about 461 tribes known as Scheduled Tribes in the country, live in this region. They are the indigenous people of Jharkhand. They are also known as *adivasis* which literally means 'Original Settlers'. Besides the Scheduled Tribes there are also other groups like the Kurmis, Tantis, Kumhars, and Tamarias etc. who have been living in this region for ages. So they also form the indigenous communities of the area.

The areas comprising Jharkhand (Bihar) was directly administered by the Governor-General until 1854, when it was placed under the charge of the Lieutenant Governor of Bengal[1]. Keeping their interest in view the British adopted a dual system of administration in Jharkhand. Part of the territory was administered directly by British officers, the rest known as Native States, were ruled over by native chiefs. However, these feudatory chiefs were not independent, for the British Government exercised a general control over their administration. But the laws that were in force in British territory did not apply to them and they were not British subjects.

Jharkhand witnessed vigorous political activity since the beginning of the nineteenth century, which manifested in the spontaneous peasant uprisings and revolts against unjust agrarian relations. Such unrest include[2] the Tamar Revolt of 1782, the Chero Uprisings of 1800-17, the Ho Uprisings of 1820-21, 1831-32, and 1837, the Kol insurrection in 1831-32, the Bhumij Revolt of 1832-34, the Santhal Hul 1855-57, the Sardar Movement of 1859-81, and the Birsa Munda Ulgulan 1895-1902.

The start of a political movement in the modern sense of the term in Jharkhand can only be traced back to the beginning of the twentieth century. The Jharkhand movement and the related political development began with the efforts of a student of St. Columbus College, Hazaribagh, an institution that became an important centre of tribal activity in the region. The pioneer was J. Bartholomew and some Anglican missionaries who established the Dacca Students Union in 1910 to deal with the problems faced by poor tribal students. The early activities of this organization were limited and ambiguous. It was a religious society, a cultural organisation, a discussion forum and a students union, all rolled into one. The Dacca Students Union planned and organized religious discourse, discussions and seminars, stage plays and represented the interests of the students. In this way the Dacca Students Union was successful in moblilizing tribal students to demand better educational facilities, economic avenues, job opportunities and so on under the leadership of J. Bartholomew and Peter Howarad[3].

Later the educated Christian tribes with active assistance from the Anglican Bishop of Ranchi reorganized the Union and re-named it the Chotanagpur Improvement Society. This new body championed the cause of adequate protection of the tribal population and their cultural identity and emphasized the pressing need to create avenues for rapid politico-economic advances of the region. In 1928, a delegation of this organization met the Simon Commission and presented the first demand for the creation of a separate province in the Jharkhand area[4].

The Chotanagpur Improvement Society was later renamed Chotanagpur Unnati Samaj in 1928. The aims of the Samaj included seeking the social, economic and political advancement of the tribals in Chotanagpur and securing for them reservation in government service and legislatures, employment for educated tribals. Removal of backwardness in the area. The Chotanagpur Unnati Samaj also played an important role in spreading political awareness against the alien rule among the people. Educated tribal leaders such as Joel Lakra, Anand Mashi Topno, Theble Oraon, Paul Dayal and Bandi Oraon led the Chotanagpur Unnati Samaj through its agenda of social reform[5].

Some leaders of the Unnati Samaj were, however, disappointed with the urban and middle class bias of their organization and were eager to make it a broad based and unified platform for the uplift and advance of tribal society. They realized that unless the land problem was made a central plank of their activities, the peasantry could not be mobilised. Some of them like Theble Oraon and Paul Dayal decided to leave the Samaj and formed the Kisan Sabha in 1931[6].

The new organisation and the Chotanagpur Unnati Samaj differed in the means of amelioration of the problems faced by the tribal population. The Kisan Sabha believed in radical action, mobilization of the peasantry to force the government to act, whereas the Chotanagpur Unnati Samaj sought deliverance through petition and memoranda[7]. The difference in their approach was akin to that between the Moderates and Extremists in the Indian National Congress in the early twentieth century. Except this difference, the leadership of the two organisations was similar.

Chotanagpur Unnati Samaj suffered further break and Baniface Lakra and Ignes Beck created the Chotanagpur Catholic Sabha with the encouragement and support of the Archbishop of Chotanagpur. The aim of this organisation was the promotion of socio-religious and economic advancement but it also took an active interest in the politics of the area. Boniface Lakra and Ignes Beck both contested the 1937 elections and were elected. The Kisan Sabha and Chotanagpur Improvement Samaj had also contested the elections, lost to the catholic candidate due to the better organisation and popularity of the Catholic Mission.

Political mobilisation took a new turn when Adivasi Mahasabha was formed in 1938 to create a Pan-tribal solidarity to resolve tribal problems. Chotanagpur Catholic Sabha, Kisan Sabha and Chotanagpur Improvement Samaj merged in the new body to convert it into a much broader Political Platform. It was at this time that Jaipal Singh joined the Adivasi Mahasabha in March-April 1939 and became its president[8]. The Adivasi Mahasabha represented a substantial advancement in the tribal politics of the Jharkhand region. It commended a wider social support base and claimed to represent Pan-tribal interests. Under the able leadership of Jaipal Singh and a band of dedicated and articulate political workers the Mahasabha soon became the representative political organisation of a large section of the people. The Mahasabha helped the war efforts of the British Government during the Second World War. Jaipal Singh himself played a key role in recruiting tribals for the British army[9].

The Adivasi Mahasabha soon spread in both rural and urban areas. It was for the first time that Sabha demanded complete separation from Bihar and the creation of a separate State. Sri Jaipal Singh who played a significant role on behalf of *adivasis* in general and Jharkhandi *adivasis* in particular in the Constituent Assembly[10]. Mahasabha had also to make a change in its composition and goal. To the leaders it became clear that this organisation could no longer ignore the non-*adivasis* living in Chotanagpur. In fact they had also been fighting for the creation of a separate State. Non-tribals of Daltonganj formed an association with Deokinandan Sinha as the first president, which placed a demand before the Parliament for converting Chotanagpur as a State[11]. So at the Jamshedpur session in 1949-50 the Mahasabha opened its doors for the non-tribals. It, however, did not deviate from the basic policy of promoting and safeguarding the interests of *adivasis.* The organisation was renamed as the Jharkhand Party. To attain this goal the Mahasabha also indulged in violent incidents (Rekhi 140-4; Sinha 283-92)[12]. The Adivasis Mahasabha decided to rename itself the Jharkhand Party in its 1949-50 sessions at Jamshedpur and extremely its membership to the non-tribal population as well. The Jharkhand Party (JP) became a full-fledged political party from 1950. Retaining it as a cultural unit of the party also preserved the identity of the Adivasis Mahasabha. Jaipal Singh became the president of the Jharkhand Party and Ignes Beck was appointed its Secretary. The Jharkhand movement gradually evolved into a full fledged regional movement both specially and demographically commanding support from all sections of the population. The movement began demanding the creation of a new province from the areas once under the Chotanagpur Division, parts of the provinces of West Bengal, Bihar, Orissa and Madhya Pradesh. An important basis for this demand was also that the entire region had been under a similar kind of administration during colonial rule[13].

During the early 1950s, Jaipal Singh campaigned for the creation of a province in Jharkhand as the only solution to the regional problem. The first General Election in 1952 showed the Jharkhand Party at the peak of popularity when it was able to secure large scale tribal as well as non-tribal support. The Jharkhand Party candidates won thirty two assembly seats and firmly established itself as the dominant political factor in the region. The culmination of this campaign was a well-attended demonstration by the tribes in 1955 at Ranchi and Dumka before the States Reorganisation Commission. The aim was to display the numerical support for a separate State. During the period 1950-57, the Jharkhand Party was able to set the agenda of politics in the Chotanagpur region. It had the ability to gather thousands of people for rallies and processions at a short notice due to the remarkable unity amongst its leaders and the party virtually laid down the law for the region during this period. The last quarter of the 1950s and the beginning of the 1960s however marked a gradual but decisive decline in the influence and power of the Jharkhand Party. The failure of Jharkhand Party to achieve the goal of a separate State led to emergence of a group of disgruntled leaders. As a result of the non-fulfilment of their demand for a separate Jharkhand State the tribals began to get disillusioned with the Jharkhand Party. In the 1957 election the number of votes polled by the Jharkhand

Party was smaller than those polled in 1952. The third General Election of 1962 came as a shock to its leaders. The number of votes polled plummeted to 4.67 lakh in 1962 as against 7.51 lakh in 1957 and 7.66 lakh in 1952. One of the reasons for the people's discontent was that the leaders were far away from them and had lost contact with the grievances of the masses[14].

## Congress-JP Merger

The leaders of the Jharkhand Party thought that their main objective of a separate Jharkhand State would only materialise if they merged with ruling Congress Party. So in September 1963, the Jharkhand Party was merged with the Congress Party. The former Chief Minister of Bihar, late Binodanand Jha, played a key role in Congress-Jharkhand Party merger. The negotiations ended in a merger agreement, which was finalized on 20 June, 1963. It stipulated that (a) a development board for Chotanagpur and Santhal Pargana and part of Bhagalpur, Moonghyr and Shahabad districts would be established to accelerate agricultural, economic, industrial and general development of the region. But the merger also proved ineffective because the general body of the Jharkhand Party had not ratified it. Jaipal Singh and others had announced the merger with the Congress Party without consulting or asking for ratification of the general body of the Jharkhand Party. (b) The Congress Party and the Jharkhand Party would merge and (c) a sub-committee of the Bihar Pradesh Congress Committee would be set up to co-ordinate political and organizational activities in the region.

One good result of the merger was that the people of Jharkhand got their first exposure to actual governmental office and day-to-day administration. Jaipal Singh was accommodated as Cabinet Minister in the Bihar Government in 1963 and all the other important leaders were appointed to various districts and State level boards.

However, the rank and file of the party was never happy with the merger of decision taken by the leaders. In fact, the decision was never ratified by the council of the party, and the leaders who had agreed to it faced a lot of criticism. The Christian tribal section also saw this merger as a threat to their influence and was, therefore, not happy with it. The merger thus encouraged more factionalism than consensus. Separate factions emerged between 1963 and 1968. Birsa Seva Dal, Krantikari Morcha and Chotanagpur Parishad.

**Birsa Seva Dal**

Birsa Seva Dal was formed by a group of young man named Lalit Kujur, Prem Kujur, Moses Guria and Pius Lakra. It was an urban group of educated tribals. In the beginning it used violent methods of struggle to secure tribal rights. Birsa Seva Dal demanded the creation of a separate State, expulsion of the Non-Chotanagpuris agrarian reforms and measures against money-lenders[15].

The activity of the Birsa Seva Dal can be roughly divided into two phases. The first phase (1967-69) was a rather extremist period in which violent means were advocate to secure the rights and better prospects for the tribal people. During this phase, large processions, guarded by tribal youths with bows and arrows, were taken out. Birsa Day was celebrated as a method of mobilizing the tribal masses. The second phase began in early 1970s when its extremist stance failed to generate any substantial following in the rural areas of the region and the influence of the leftist party waned. It, therefore, decided to restrict itself to adopt constitutional methods to pursue its demands.

**Emergence of JMM**

From 1972, onwards the Jharkhand movement began to take a new turn. For the first time both the industrial workers and the peasants came together to fight against the exploitation they were undergoing. The struggle began to take the form of a class struggle. On 4 February, 1973, at Dhanbad the Sonat Santhal Samaj of Shibu Soren and the Shibaji Samaj led by Binod Bihari Mahato merged together and formed the Jharkhand

Mukti Morcha (JMM)[16]. The ideological force behind the Morcha was the trade union leader A.K. Roy of the Marxist Coordination Committee. The Morcha combined in its operations elements of agrarian radicalism and cultural revivalism. It launched an operation to recover alienated lands from money-lenders and big peasants. After its formation, it organized forcible harvesting of crops standing on lands illegally taken from *adivasis*, Kurmis, Harijans and poor Muslims by the money-lenders. The Morcha also tried to remove the social evils like drinking from tribal society. For the development of tribals it took up co-operative farming and literacy programmes. Under the leadership of JMM the tribal peasants, landless labourers and industrial workers started a popular movement against exploitation on all the four fronts. These were :

1. Recovery of land illegally taken from the tribals by the money-lenders and *mahajans*,
2. Obtaining employment for local tribals in the public undertaking established in the area. The Morcha started an *andolan* to get proper compensation for the land to be taken from the tribals for the construction of big projects like Koel-Karo Project in Ranchi District and Subarnarekha Multi Purpose Project in West Singhbhum District.
3. The *Jungal Katai Anadolan* against the anti-people forest policy of the Government.
4. The formation of a separate Jharkhand State. In the beginning the Morcha operated under the leadership of triumvirate—A.K. Roy, Binod Bihari Mahato among the Kurmi peasants and Shibu among the tribals. Although they co-ordinated their activities they could not forge a united front effectively.

Efforts were also made towards political mobilization on the basis of leftist ideology.

The JMM and the MCOR (The Marxist Co-Ordination Committee) established the Jharkhand Alliance between the workers and peasants, since, according to them, a 'Jharkhandi' was any one who worked and a *'diku'* was any one who exploited others. Their aim was to unite all Jharkhandis against all *dikus* to ensure the creation of a separate State of Jharkhand. The JMM led the alliance with the slogan 'Jharkhand Lalkhand'. Processions and rallies organized under the joint leadership of the JMM and the MCOR soon drew up to fifty thousand people, and they demand for a separate Jharkhand[17].

## The Forest *Andolan* in Singhbhum—1978

In the year 1978, the Kolhan Porahat area of Singhbhum District witnessed the outbreak of a well-organised movement known as the *Jungle Katai Andolan* started by the Adivasis of this area is closely linked to the natural resources and the environment amidst which they live. They have the total right on the part of the 'Mother Earth'. They have developed various norms, values, beliefs and practices which regulate the use of the natural resources around them in such a way that nature always remained beautiful to them. The *adivasis* have a special relationship to the land they hold. The land provides assurance for their continued survival. It is the land that gives life and meaning to their whole being, for it is in their land that their history and identity are contained. That is why for the *adivasis* land and blood are homologous. Their society, culture, religion, identity and their very existence are intimately linked to the land they hold[18].

The *Andolan* took the form of felling of trees in the forests, by the *adivasis* as a symbolic protest against the threat to their livelihood and identity. It spread like wild fire in the whole area and vast areas of forest were cut down by the *adivasis.* Their argument was that these lands once belonged to them and were illegally taken away by the Forest Department[19]. The movement for a separate Jharkhand State was also renewed and intensified during this period. It was inspired by the statements made by Jay Prakash Narayan about the advisability and need for reorganisation and formation of small States. Immediately after this the movement for a separate State was intensified by all the political parties and they formed a 'United Front' to achieve their aim. The movement in Singhbhum was led by Deven Majhi of JMM.

## The Emergence of the Kolhan Raksha Sangh[20]

For the first time in the history of tribal movement in Jharkhand an attempt to form an independent nation for the Hos of Kolhan (Singhbhum) was made by an organization called the Kolhan Raksha Sangh. Their demand for a separate nation, consisting of a part of Singhbhum was based on the peculiar system of administration, which exists in this area. During the British time the Kolhan was a Government Estate. The administration of this area was done according to the Wilkinson's Rules which made use of the indigenous Munda-Manki system. Civil justice was administered accordingly to the rules without recourse to civil courts. Mundas and Mankis were responsible for land settlement and general superintendence over the village revenue system.

On 30 October, 1977 a combined meeting of the Kolhan Raksha Sangh and the Kolhan-Porahat Munda-Manki Sangh was held at Chaibasa which discussed the aims of the Kolhan Raksha Sangh. According to Narayan Jonko, the founder and chief of the Kolhan Raksha Sangh started the aims were :

1. The Kolhan Raksha Sangh will largely be a policy making body and will also review the Right of Wilkinson's Rules and Mankis and Mundas as well as *raiyats* and make necessary suggestions to the Central Government.
2. The Kolhan Raksha Sangh shall also organize conference and seminars from time to time and also research work regarding the conduct of the Kolhan Administration Programme.

On 30 March, 1981, the Kolhan Raksha Sangh held a meeting at the Chaibasa market during which the speakers proclaimed that Kolhan had not been part of British India ruled by the Viceroy from Delhi, that the Indian Parliament had no power to pass laws for Kolhan and that Kolhan was a sovereign state. The leaders also remarked that the matter would be taken to the UNO[21].

## Formation of the All Jharkhand Students Union

The active involvement of students in the movement for separate Jharkhand State has been on different occasions. These were :

1. In 1966-67, when the students joined hands with the Birsa Seva Dal movement,
2. 1974-75 in the occasion of the J. P. Movement under the leadership of Salkhan Murmu and Karma Oraon.

On June 22, 1986, under the leadership of Surya Singh Besra, AJSU was formed. In 1986 Besra, with the help of Nirmal Mahto organised a conference of intellectuals and students at Jamshedpur. AJSU put forward two important proposals :

1. Boycott of elections until Jharkhand is obtained,
2. A time-bound plan of action to obtain Jharkhand.

At present AJSU has become an important factor in the Jharkhand Movement through its radical actions like calling of Bandh, economic blockade etc. The AJSU since its inception had been the most vocal constituent. It had been giving out calls for blockading of all mineral mining and transportation in the Jharkhand region to force the Union Government to agree to the formation of the State of Jharkhand as well as to secure a better policy response to the development problems of the region. On 8 August, 1987, Nirmal Mahato, the president of JMM was murdered at Jamshedpur[22]. This led to a agitation in Singhbhum area.

## Formation of the Jharkhand Coordination Committee (1987)

In order to establish a common front, a conference of delegates of all political, social, cultural and literary organisations supporting the Jharkhand Movement was held at Ramgarh from 11 to 13 September, 1987. It was attended by 429 delegates who represented 49 organisations. The Jharkhand Coordination Committee (JCC) was formed at this conference and Dr. B.P. Kesari was appointed its Convenor with JCC's efforts a new wave of intellectual participation emerged giving the movement of sense of maturity[23]. Under Kesari's leadership the most significant aspect of the development of the movement was the gradual involvement of the Sadan population of the Jharkhand area. The JMM also joined forces with the JCC in the larger interest of the movement.

However, the euphoria generated by the unity proved short lived with the JMM insisting on a greater say in organizational matters by virtue of its being the single largest constituent of JCC. With the JCC leadership under Kesari reluctant to award greater representation to the JMM in the organizational set-up, JMM finally quit the JCC. The Committee, as a consequence, failed to hold together on its own and differences surfaced between the AJSU and the JCC constituents, as the AJSU leadership wanted to establish control over the committee. On their own, the AJSU, the JMM and the JCC decided to go ahead with demonstrations to press their demand for a separate State. The result was that at present the JCC almost become defunct.

In 1989, AJSU raised the slogan "No Elections without Jharkhand" and called for boycott of all elections until Jharkhand was achieved. It had a little impact on the Lok Sabha elections. As a result, AJSU changed this policy and decided to join the election policies. For this purpose on 31 December, 1991, the Jharkhand People Party (JPP) was formed as an associate political party of AJSU. Dr. Ram Dayal Munda was chosen as the first president of the party and Surya Singh Besara as its chief secretary[24].

## Demand for a Separate Vananchal State by the BJP

The BJP for the first time practically hijacked the issue of a Jharkhand State in Election Manifesto of 1991 with its demand for Vananchal. The leaders of JMM and other Jharkhandi Parties had a vision of a Jharkhand State comprising twenty five districts from four States Bihar, Orissa, Madhya Pradesh and West Bengal. The BJP on the other hand, proposed the creation of a State called Vananchal with 18 districts of South Bihar only. The new proposal of the BJP offered an alternative that was simpler to implement. In August 1989, a Committee on Jharkhand Matters (COJM) was formed. The COJM was asked to examine and recommend modalities for meeting the just aspirations of the region within the framework of the Constitution. The Committee submitted its report to the Union Home Minister in 18 May, 1990, suggesting three possible solutions to the Jharkhand problem—(1) Statehood, (2) Union Territory, (3) Jharkhand General Council within the State of Bihar.

After the Assembly elections of 1990, the JMM won 19 seats in the State Assembly out of 82 seats and six Lok Sabha seats of the Jharkhand area and emerged as the strongest party in Jharkhand. Janata Dal formed the government with the support of BJP and JMM. The Janata Dal Government in Bihar under Laloo Prasad Yadav pushed through in the Bihar Assembly a bill on the formation of the Jharkhand Area Development Council. Soon, Union Home Minister, S.B. Chavan announced that provided the four Chief Ministers of Bihar, Orissa, Madhya Pradesh and West Bengal agreed the Centre might not be averse to the formation of a separate Jharkhand State. The Centre requested the four Chief Ministers to meet on 18 February, 1992. But it was Laloo Yadav and Jyoti Basu who made it. From March, 1992, the different Jharkhand groups decided on going ahead with their agitational programmes, *bandhs* and economic blockades to create pressure on the Centre. The Centre agreed to place a summary of the COJM (Committee on Jharkhand Matters) report in Parliament. The report was placed in Parliament in March 1992.[25]

Meanwhile the JMM split on the issue of selection of Subodh Kant Sahay as the nominee of the JMM for Rajya Sabha elections. A group led by Krishna Mardi opposed the move and supported the Laloo Government. The other group led by

Shibu Soren supported the move and decided to withdraw support. It was at this juncture that the Union Home Minister announced at the end of August 1992 that a decision on Jharkhand would be taken in a fortnight's time. On 8 September, 1992 the Home Minister surprisingly stated that the only way out of the impasse was to grant Union Territory or separate State status to Jharkhand.

On 9 August, 1995, the Jharkhand Area Autonomous Council was sworn in. No election was held for the election of the council members. During the General Elections to the Parliament held in 1995, the BJP won most of the seats from the Jharkhand area[26].

In the mean time, the involvement of some of the JMM MPs including Shibu Soren, Suraj Mandal and others in a corruption case undermined their position. As a result the case of separate statehood appeared to loose force. But the BJP took up the cause and became very active on the demand of a separate State. The year 1997 transformed the political scenario in Bihar. Laloo Prasad Yadav involved in multi-crore animal husbandry fodder scam, and he was arrested. All these factors caused a split in the Janata Dal and Laloo Prasad Yadav formed a new party called the Rastriya Janata Dal (RJD). In order to survive, the RJD government secured the support of JMM MLAs. In return the latter managed to get a resolution passed on 23 July, 1997 in the Assembly recommending for the creation of a separate State[27].

The BJP led National Democratic Alliance (NDA) came to power at the Centre after the 1999 Lok Sabha elections. The BJP had secured 11 out of 14 Lok Sabha seats of Jharkhand; one seat went to the RJD and the remaining two to Congress. As a result the National Democratic Alliance fulfilled its electoral promise of a separate State by passing the State Reorganisation Bill 2000 from Lok Sabha on 2 August, 2000. After passage by the Rajya Sabha and approval of the President of India, the new State of Jharkhand came into being on 15 November, 2000.[28] Prabhat Kumar became the first Governor of Jharkhand and Babulal Marandi the first Chief Minister of the new State.

## Conclusion

Thus the creation of a new Jharkhand State is a result of continuous struggle of indigenous people. Jharkhand emerged as the 28th State of India in the mid-night of 14th November 2000. Though a new State has been created but ruling alliance has done much damage to the Jharkhandi and particularly *adivasi* people. At the economic level industrializing and mining in *avidasi* land was being encouraged thus paving the way for capitalist industrialists to flourish in the mineral rich region. The needs of Jharkhandi farmers for irrigation of the people in basic health and rural education are completely and deliberately neglected.

### REFERENCES


1. M. Sahu, *The Kolhan under the British Rule,* Calcutta, p. 61, 1985.
2. S.K. Singh, *Inside Jharkhand,* Ranchi, p. 63.
3. *Ibid.,* Inside Jharkhand, Ranchi, p. 64.
4. B.N.P. Sinha *Jharkhand, Land and People,* Rajesh Publication, Delhi.
5. *Ibid.,*
6. *Ibid.,* S.K. Singh, p. 66.
7. S.K. Singh, *Inside Jharkhand,* Ranchi, p. 66.
8. R.K. Tiwary, *Jharkhand Ki Roop Rekha,* Ranchi, p. 185.
9. *Struggled for Jharkhand,* Mathew Aree Parampill S.J., p. 240.
10. *Ibid.,* p. 240.
11. S.K. Singh., *Inside Jharkhand Ranchi,* p. 69.
12. Rekhi., 140, Sinha, 83-92.
13. *Struggled for Jharkhand,* Mathew Aree Parampill, S. J., p. 241.
14. *Struggle for Jharkhand,* Mathew Aree Parampill S. J., p. 242.
15. Prakash, Amit, 2001, *Jharkhand Politics of Development and Identity,* New Delhi, Nunes Publication, p. 107.
16. Abua Raj, 2000b, *Swaraj Ke Liya Jharkhandiyon Ka Ek Sangharsh—Ek Sankshipt Itihas,* Chaibasa Tribal Research and Taining Centre.
17. Balbir Dutt, *Kahani Jharkhand Adnolan Ki,* Crown Publication, Ranchi, 2005, p. 407.
18. M. Areeparampil, *Forest Andolan in Singhbhum,* in S. Narayan (ed), *Jharkhand Movements: Origin and Evolution,* Inter India Publication, New Delhi, p. 149.
19. C.K. Paty, *Jungle Katai Andolan* (1978) and Singhbhum in Paty (ed.) *Forest, Government and Tribe,* p. 98.

20. *Struggled for Jharkhand*—M. Areeparampill, S.J., pp. 256-257.
21. *Struggled for Jharkhand,* M Areeparampill, pp. 257-259.
22. *Prabhat Khabar,* 9 Aug 1987, Ranchi.
23. Balbir Dutt, *Kahani Jharkhand Andolan Ki,* Crown Publication Ranchi, 2005, p. 411.
24. *Ibid.,* p. 414.
25. Mathew Areeparampil, *Struggle for Swaraj,* pp. 262-263.
26. Balbir Dutt, *Kahani Jharkhand Andolan Ki,* Crown Publication, Ranchi 2005 p. 456.
27. S.K. Singh, *Inside Jharkhand,* Crown Publication, Ranchi, 2006, p. 77.
28. Balbir Dutt, *Kahani Jharkhand Andolan Ki,* Crown Publication, Ranchi 2005, p. 462.

# 11

# Assertion of Identity over *Jal, Jungle* and *Jameen* in Singhbhum 1947–2007

LALITA SUNDI

The district of Singhbhum is situated in the south of Jharkhand between 21°58′ and 23°36′ north latitude and between 85°5′ and 86°54′ east longitude[1]. The name Singhbhum, that is, the *land of the Singhs* is most probably derived from the patronymic of the Rajas of Porahat, to whom the north of the district was once subject. Another theory is that the name is a corruption of *Sing Bonga* the principal God-head of the *Hos,* the *adivasis* of Singhbhum district[2].

The *Ho* tribe of Singhbhum was once part of the *Munda* tribe and they lived with them in the Chotanagpur plateau. Gradually, the *Hos,* who preferred to remain independent left the parent tribe when they had chosen their king and migrated to the south-east of Chotanagpur about 10th century A.D.[3] In course of migration they first settled in the Tebo *ghat* areas of the present day Bandagaon block of Singhbhum district. The *Hos* once settled in these *ghat* areas is evident from the numerous villages whose names correspond to the names of Ho *Kilis* (*gotras*). From there they slowly migrated into the Singhbhum plains. It is believed that the *Saraks* or *Srawaks,* i.e., the Lay *Jainas* were the first settlers of this area. The *Bhuiyans* and then *Hos* were the next settlers. *Hos* first penetrated into north Singhbhum, cleared jungles, settled villages as *Khuntkattidars* (original settlers) and gradually moved southwards from Porahat area to Singhbhum plains from where some of these gradually entered Orissa. Singhbhum became their permanent home.[4] Here they cleared forests only according to their needs. They had established their villages according to their *Kilis* and for their village administration they organised *Manki-Munda* system. In 1837, Captain Thomas Wilkinson, the Agent of the *South-West Frontier Agency* subjugated *Ho* dominated parts of Singhbhum and made it a different administrative unit known as *Kolhan Government Estate.*[5] He had recognised the *Manki Munda* system of administration of this area. In this traditional system of administration *Munda* was the head of his village. Some villages further constituted a larger unit known as *Pir* (a group of villages). The head of the *Pir* was *Manki*. These *Mundas* and *Mankis* were given police powers. They were responsible for land settlements and general superintendence over the village revenue system.[6] This system of administration still exists in this area.

The *Hos* are closely linked to nature. Its resources such as *jal, jungle* and *jameen* supported life as well as spirituality. The *jameen* or land provides assurance for their continued survival. The *jameen* is also a symbol of their history and identity because it contains their *sasan* (burial places of their ancestors) and their *sasandiri* (huge stone placed on the graves). These *sasans* are signs that once *Ho* lived there. They maintain that *sasans* are their *Kurshinama* (*vanshavali*) bacause every family has its *sasan* only in its own land.So they have emotional and religious link with the *sasan* also. Ownership of land is not individual. It belongs to the community. So it cannot be sold or transferred, except by inheritance. It has social, cultural, religious and existential value in the context of this region.[7]

The *Hos* have been worshippers of nature *ab initio.* They deify *Sing Bonga* (sun), *Marang Buru* (god of mountain), *Desauli* (village tutelary god), *Marang Bonga* (great god), and *Nage Bonga* (river diety) besides other manifestations of divinity. The *Sing Bonga* is the Supreme God of the *Hos*. The *Marang Bonga* is the presiding deity of the original home of the *Hos*. Every village has a sacred grove (cluster of Sarjom or Sal tree) called

*Sarna* or *Jahira* at the outskirt of the village. It was supposed to be the abode of the village tutelary god *Desauli* and *Jahira Burhi,* his consort. No one may pluck leaves of the tree or cut its branches, fell it or plough the land under it[8].

*Jal* is essential for human-being for their survival. When *Hos* came to Singhbhum, they had settled by rivers in order to have water for livelihood and cattle. They get fishes and many other things from water as their food. For the importance of water the *Hos* began to worship it. *Nage Bonga* is the river deity. She is known as the wife of *Sing Bonga.* She is believed to have some place of abode inside the river. They believed that wherever these are *Nage Bonga,* water never dries up. As it seldom known where she actually dwells, the *Hos* do not disturb the water by throwing stones into it and do not make the water dirty.[9]

The *Jungle* is the very centre of tribal life. Their material and religious life depend upon it. They make the objects of their daily life from different trees, grass, ropes and timber of the forests. It supplies wood for their fuel. It also provides fodder, water and shelter to their domesticated animals. After hunting wild animals and different birds from jungle, they eat them. They get an important supplementry diet from fruits, leaves and flowers of trees. They also get honey, mushroom and herbs from jungle.[10] Their festivals like *Baha Parab* is celebrated only after getting branches of *Sal* or *Sarjom* tree (*Shorea robusta*) and flowers from the jungle. The *Hos* also use forests as their means of livelihood. They cultivate *Tassar* and *Lac* on different trees. *Lac* is grown on *Kusum (Schleicheratrijuga). Palas, Pipal* and *Bair* trees and *Tassar Cocoons* are grown on *asan (Terminalia tomentosa)* and *sal* trees[11]. They also obtain oil from fruit seeds of *Mahua (Bassia latefolia), Kusum, Karanj (Pongomia glabra)* and *Neem (Melia indica).*[12]

In this way, the people of Singhbhum have developed innate and reciprocal relationship with *jal, jungle* and *jameen* situated around them. On the one hand to safeguard their existence, they cleared the jungles to establish their villages, make houses and prepare lands for agriculture and also tried to get additional income from them for their livelihood, on the other hand their dependence, affection and respect are expressed through their religion, adoration and festivals. In this way the *Hos* have lived peacefully in Singhbhum by consumption of *jal, jungle* and *jameen* since times immemorial.

During British period frequent encroachments upon these sources of live have given birth to movement since 1819-20 (Ho Rebellion). In 1836-37 (Kolhan Rebellion) the *Hos* put up a fierce fight against the British.[13] Similarly, during the revolt of 1857, they also rose against foreign dominion.[14] But later they seemed to rationalise with the foreign domination and live peacefully under the British rule. But from the colonial records, it becomes evident that discontent was simmering within against the transgression of their customary rights.

The British framed different forest rules to have more and more revenue but they did not bother for the vital interests of the tribals. By Notification of 10 August, 1875 (under Act VII of 1865) *Saranda Pir* was declared Reserved Forest.[15] Outside the reserved forest, all forests were known as the village forests, which were enjoyed by the *raiyats* subject to the control of the village headmen (Munda-Manki). Under the Notification No. 3375 of 5 September, 1892 all unreserved forests were made protected forests by the Government. During Craven settlement of 1895-97, 58 forest blocks were demarcated and in 1903 the remaining areas were declared to be the village forests. During Tucky settlement of 1913-18 there were 331 villages with protected forests. These new rules contravened people's existing rights of collecting timber, forest produce and of grazing cattle subject only to the control of their *Munda-Manki*. This step derived *adivasi* of their age-old rights to jungle. On the other hand, private companies were allowed to exploit forest produce and minerals. Grazing taxes were imposed in 1922.[16] Similarly *Indian Forest Act, 1927* curtailed *Manki-Munda's* traditional power and jurisdiction and encroached upon the customary forest rights of the tribals, thereby creating a situation of conflict and confrontation.[17]

The same practice of discrimination and injustice continued with promulgation of *Bihar Private Forest Act, 1947.* This Act prohibited tribals against cutting trees for purposes of fuel, cut, collect or removes timber etc. for domestic or agricultural needs and reclaims land in forest for the purpose of cultivation.[18] *National Forest Policy 1952* also prohibited tribals to use forest products for their domestic and agricultural need.[19] In 1973, the Bihar Government nationalised the *kendu* leaves trade by the Bihar Kendu Leaves (Control of Trade) Act. 1973.[20] Similarly in 1975, the Bihar State Forest Development Corporation Ltd *(FDC)* was set up for the purpose of commercial exploitation of forests. An area of 39,968 hectares of Porahat Forest Division was leased out by the FDC. The Corporation began to replace *Sal, Mahua, Kusum* and other useful and fruit bearing trees by teak (sagwan) in the traditional mixed forests which included *Khuntkatti* forests in which *adivasis* have complete rights. Thus vast areas of natural mixed forests on which the tribal communities depended for their survival were cleared and felled and replaced by monoculture of commercially useful species such as *teak.* During 30 years, forest department used the agricultural land of *adivasi* in illegal way by adding them as land of forest and like this, most *adivasis* had lost their lands. They were forced out of their *Khuntkatti* villages. They left behind them the *Sasan, Sasandiri, Desauli,* the *paddy fields* which they had made and the *mango* and *tamarind* trees which they had planted as signs that once they lived there. Due to which the social, religious and cultural activities of *adivasi* had also been damaged.[21]

Similarly in 1976, Bihar Government took over the sal seeds trade and in 1978 trade in all minor forest produce was also taken over by the Government.[22] All these Acts or laws are against the tribals. Sometimes, Government officials sexually exploited their women also. There were large scale legal and illegal alienation of tribal land, displacement of tribals due to various projects like Tata Steel Company (Jamshedpur, 1907), Associate Cement Company, Jhinkpani (1946) and Subarnarekha Multi Purpose Project (1982) without proper rehabilitation and adequate compensation. In this area also increasing unemployment due to the closure of mines and frequent drought in the area.[23] Unemployment increased sky-high, leading to mass discontent and resentment.

These factors were responsible for militant movements in August 1978, known as *Jungle Andolan* in Singhbhum. This *Andolan* spread quickly to Kolhan, Porahat and in the dense forest of Saranda. The leaders of different Jharkhand parties like *Jharkhand Party, Jharkhand Mukti Morcha,* and *Singhbhum Jungle Mazdoor Union* etc. participated in this movement. The movement for a separate Jharkhand State was also renewed and intensified during this period. The *Jungle Andolan* for reclaiming land for cultivation was first started by *Machua Gagrai* in the Karaikela area who had organised about 67 villages for this movement. They had been reclaiming the lands which once belonged to their ancestors but had been taken over by the Forest Department.[24] *Devan Majhi* and *Shailendra Mahto* of *Singhbhum Jungle Mazdoor Union* were the leaders of *Jungle Andolan.* In the next phase *Shailendra Mahato* started *Sagwan Katai Andolan* in the Serengda area. This *andolan* spread in the forest area of Sonua, Goilkera, Manoharpur, Bandgaon and Chakradharpur like wild fire. All the teak plants were uprooted, huts in the nurseries were burnt down and costly pump sets belonging to FDC were destroyed. After destroying the teak plants the tribals started ploughing the area for cultivation.[25] On 6 November, 1978, a meeting was held at Ichahatu village in Goilkera block, the police indiscriminately fired at a crowd of *adivasis* in which *Maheswar Jamuda* of Nugri village died and *Antu Marla* was wounded.[26] In the same year in Serengda firing *Nupa Bur* and their two friends died on the spot and many were seriously injured. On 1 December, 1978, *Devendra Majhi* was arrested at Chakradharpur. On the same day the police raided Lonjo village in search of *Shailendra Mahto.* Not finding him there, the police harassed the villagers including women.[27] There were several cases of police firing in the whole of Singhbhum. Therefore, on 1979, a Committee named People's Union for Civil Liberties and Democratic Rights, Delhi came to Singhbhum to investigate the incidents of atrocities committed on *adivasis.*[28]

In spite of all these repression the *andolan* continued with vigour. In the mean time on 4 September, 1980 about 158 tribals were arrested at Goilkera on the charge of cutting the forest.

Thus wherever this movement gathered momentum, repression was started by the police. This was the reason why *Bihar Military Police (BMP)* was deployed throughout the forest area but these forces harassed the tribals in several ways. The cruelty of police reached its peak at Gua on 8 September 1980, where due to the police suppression, a meeting was organised. 11 tribals were killed in police firing and 4 policemen were killed by the arrows of *adivasis.* Even patients admitted to hospitals for treatment were killed. *Ramo Laguri, Chungi, Chando Laguri, Chungi Rogo, Suren Kutumbia, Bagi Deogam, Jilu Soren, Chetan Champia, Jura Purty, Budu Gondo Honhaga, Ishwar Chandra Sardar* etc. were killed.[29] Further, on 24 November, 1980 in Baipi village of Chakradharpur, *Dutia Honhaga* and in the same year, *Tikur Lagury* of Kuira village were killed in police firing. In 1981, *Topa Hembram* of Sarjomhatu was also killed in police firing. Thus there was a long list of victims of police firing, who fought for their rights.[30]

The most inhuman and brutal of all these killings is the murder of *Gangaram Kalundia* in police custody. He was an ex-army man who had won the *President Award* for bravery. After his retirement he was organizing the people of his area for getting just compensation for the lands to be taken away from them for construction of the *Subarnarekha Multi Purpose* Project. On 4 April, 1982, he was brutally killed by police.[31] Similarly in 1983, *Bidar Nag* of Gua, who was also an ex-army man, was killed by police. Like this in a small span of time from 1978 to 1985, 18 police firings happened in which many innocent *adivasis* were killed. *Chief Judicial Magistrate of Singhbhum* on 14 April 1987 sent a report to *Supreme Court of India* according to which 5,160 cases were pending in different courts on 14,000 *adivasis.* Some of the cases were pending since 1960.[32] All these incidents made the movement more aggressive.

People's struggle for *jal, jungle* and *jameen* did not stop here. Several leaders, like *Lal Singh Munda* (1984), *Nirmal Mahto* (1987) and *Machua Gagrai* (1989) were the other martyrs of this movement. A great tribal leader, *Devendra Majhi* who was on the target of contractors and policemen, was killed on 14 October, 1994 at Goilkera *hat.* After that many incidents of fight between *adivasis* and police occurred.

However, this movement later on gradually became weakened because the leaders did not care for the victims of police atrocities. At the same time some leaders left this movement and joined some other party for election purposes. Thus for the lack of proper leadership this *andolan* came to an end.[33]

During this time Jharkhand Movement was continued in different phases and finally on 15 November, 2000 new Jharkhand State was constituted. Jharkhand was declared as the 28th State of India.[34] The tribals of the State believed that now their rights over *jal, jungle* and *jameen* must be recognised but in vain. Their dreams were broken. In the name of development and industrialisation all State Government followed anti-tribal policies and the tribals were displaced from their lands. Therefore, the tribals started to raise their voice against displacement.

In course of time several organisations came into existence in the whole of Singhbhum in defence of their rights. Formerly, these organisations alone raised their voice against injustice. But after some time, they realised that loud voice can be raised against any kind of injustice collectively. So 10 big organisations of the district constituted a larger organisation named *Macha Kumuti (Co-ordination of Public Organisations)* on 14 October, 2005. These organisations were *Adivasi Ho Samaj Mahasabha, Kolhan Porahat Manki-Munda Sangh, Manki-Munda Committee Chakradharpur, Kolhan Raksha Sangh, Kolhan Porahat Visthapan Pratirodhi Adivasi Sangathan, Gram Ganhrajya Jila Samiti, Jharkhand Mines Area Co-ordination Committee (JMACC), Yuva Jumur West Singhbhum, Mahila Sandarbh Kendra Chaibasa* and *Johar Chaibasa. Macha Kumuti* organised a mammoth *Aakrosh Ekta Rally* in Gandhi Maidan, Chaibasa on 10 November, 2005.[35] Armed with traditional weapons the workers of several organisations took out a historical rally and submitted memorandum to the *Divisional Commissioner* of the Kolhan division in the name of the *President of India* and the *Governor of Jharkhand.* These are the demands of the memorandum.

To

His Excellency
The President of India
New Delhi
and
His Excellency
The Governor
State of Jharkhand

| | | |
|---|---|---|
| Through | : | Commissioner, Kolhan Division, Chaibasa, West Singhbhum, Jharkhand. |
| Sub | : | Ban of land acquisition for national and multinational companies for establishing industries in the Notified Scheduled Areas. |
| Context | : | Non-compliance and non-implementation of the provisions of the Constitution of India (Articles—224(1) and Fifth Schedule), Chotanagpur Tenancy Act 1908, Panchayat Extension in Scheduled Area Act 1996 (PESA), Judgments of Supreme Court of India (Samta Judgments) and non-compliance of the National Tribal Policy of the Ministry of Tribal Welfare, Government of India. |

His Excellency,

With regard to the above mentioned subject, we the notified tribes/original dwellers/aboriginals oppose the land acquisition in Schdule Areas for projects of heavy industrialisation due to following reasons :

1. Considering the provision in *Part XXII* of the Constitution, enshrined there in the *FIFTH SCHEDULE,* where special provisions have been made for the administration and control of the Scheduled Areas. The Governor is the sole custodian of the Scheduled Areas and any regulation made requires mandatory approval by the *Tribal Advisory Council.* It is this aspect of the Constitution which is been overlooked

while signing MoU (Memorandum of Understanding) with the Private Industrial Corporate. If execution of any MoU takes place, displacement of the poor and illiterate tribals is inevitably causing misery and even their extinction.

2. In conformity with the *Fifth Schedule* para 5, sub-para 2, *Bihar Scheduled Area Regulation, 1969* (Section 71 A of CNT) for proper and good governance was made. Under this regulation, the tribal lands acquired illegally/fraudulently by non tribals are to be restored back to its original owners. On contrary to this, the State Government by implementing wrong policies, is causing tribal displacement and affecting their integrity and their very existence.
3. The possession of traditional tribal ancestral lands is immemorial and self created property. This possession came much before the creation of state or country. So, therefore, the tribal land is considered non-transferable and is retained by the same family clan from generation to generation and, therefore, is owned by the entire village which is the tradition and custom. As landed property is self creation by the original settlers and as not given or allotted by the State Government, their lands should not be acquired by the State. Only those lands which were given to the tribals after the State came into existence could be acquired by the State only for public purpose.
4. The Supreme Court of India, in its historic Judgments (Samta Judgment 1997), clearly states instruction and guidelines for the non-transfer of tribal lands or any lease thereof to any non-tribal for the purpose of mining or any other projects. Even the State is also banned from acquiring the *raiyati* lands from the tribals in the Scheduled Area. Irony is that the State Government makes all efforts to acquire tribal lands in the Scheduled Area in favour of the national and multinational companies, without caring for the welfare policies the Constitution and the instruction of the Supreme Court of India.
5. As per the CNT Act, Sec. 50 (1) no Deputy Commissioner can acquire the *jaher sthan* and other place of worship and burial place because the *CNT Act* do not permit it. There is

not a single village where there is no place of worship as indicated by the Act. In addition to it, there is only arable land under this Act, which cannot be acquired for the industrial purpose and alienate them for non-agricultural activity.

6. It is forbidden to acquire land without the written consent of tribal *raiyats* as per *CNT Act.* So overlooking this aspect of the Act, the Secretary of Industry and Deputy Commissioner, making land available or acquiring for establishing industries as agreement with the State is in violation of the Act.
7. It is essential to consult village bodies (Gram Sabha) before acquiring the land as per Section 4 (7) of the *Panchayat Extension in Scheduled Area Act 1996*. The Government has made it prestige issue by violating it with a view to displace countless villages for setting up industry.
8. The *Tribal National Policy* proposed by the *Ministry of Tribal Welfare, Government of India,* is strictly against the displacement of the tribes from their ancestral land as this is in violation of the Fifth Schedule of the Constitution. In gross violation of the provision, the Government surveys are made to acquire land for the industrial corporates.
9. After numerous agreement signed with industrial houses, the governmental machinery is offering assurance and making statement that industrial houses would provide proper compensation and employment facility. This would lead to all-round development of the area and improvement in the people's standard of living. How far these officials' statements are true can be clearly seen with the ground realities from the facts mentioned below :—

   (a) Ever since after the Independence there have been far reaching consequences on our population as a result of establishing factories, mines, water projects and firing range for the army on our tribal lands. Our population has gone down from 70 per cent to 21 per cent in every census made after the gap of every ten years. So by establishing 41 big industries, our population is bound to disappear.

(b) The other facts is, the Government has not yet paid compensation to lakhs of people displaced in the name of projects. According to *Indian Social Institute, New Delhi*, 6 lakhs tribals have been displaced by governmental and non-governmental projects in Jharkhand alone. They have not been rehabilitated. They are roaming here and there with futureless existence as paupers and beggars. In the light of this fact the Government's assurance is nothing more than a joke with tribals.

(c) As per report of *Indian Bureau of Mines 1974*, in the Kolhan Division 40 small and big factories and 300 mines are there, and 4 towns have become 24 towns. If today *Mittal, Jindal* and *Essar* are allowed to make another Tata, Bokaro or Dhanbad, the situation of the tribal will only worsen causing more adversity.

(d) The number of tribal/original workers at Tata and A.C.C Jhinkpani is negligible. So the assurance of employment to displaced persons by the Government is baseless and unconvincing.

(e) Tribals have not yet been given the benefit of reservations in governmental works in Bokaro, H.E.C., Hatia, Kiriburu, Gua and Chiria (where official reservation policy is in force). In such a case the question of providing employment to displaced tribals does not arise in the proposed private industries which are not under the control of reservation policy.

10. Apart from these our population is suffering day by day because of the governmental policies, which must be put to a halt. In this regard:-

(i) All the cases regarding encroachment on forest land in the Scheduled Areas of Jharkhand under *Indian Forest Act* should be immediately withdrawn. The forest land, on which tribals are residing after being displaced, should be settled with these as notified revenue villages.

(ii) *Land Requisition Act* and *Delimitation Act* should not be enforced in Scheduled Areas keeping the decreasing tribals population in mind (in the light of the Fifth Schedule of the Constitution).

(iii) Tribal lands are the property, created naturally and acquired by them having perpetual rights, which existed much prior to creation of modern state or country. Thereby issuance of temporary, local residential certificate by the State Government to tribal's despite verification of their land records will only mean diminishing their identity that should be stopped without delay[36].

Thus this mammoth rally has proved that *adivasis* have become more vigilant about their right to *jal, jungle* and *jameen* and they will not let themselves deprived of their rights at any cost.

In these days several villages and organisations continued to protest against the acquisition of land for several projects. *Bhumi Raksha Sangh* of Cherai Pir, picketed before the circle office Chaibasa on 8 December, 2007 against the land acquisition for *Essar Integrated Steel Plant Limited.*[37] Similarly, the villagers of Matagutu in Jhinkpani block protested against the plan for setting up of cement plant by *Messrs Jupiter Cement Industries.* On 24 December 2007 the villagers of Bara Guira picketed before Chaina Clay Quarry for its closer.[38]

In this way we see that the history of Singhbhum is the history of perpetual and unceasing struggle of the *adivasi* for the protection of their right over *jal, jungle* and *jameen*. In this place are situated their holy *Desauli, Jahersthan, Sasandiri, Marang Bonga, Ading, Nagesude* etc., which are the identity of the society, religion and culture of the *adivasis*. After the formation of separate State Jharkhand the people were convinced that their right to *jal, jungle* and *jameen* will be recognised but it did not come true. On the other hand, those who protested against the land acquisition were declared the enemy of development. Is development possible only at the cost of *adivasis*? Is this the real definition of development? For their right to *jal, jungal* and *jameen* and for their entity the struggle of adivasi will gather momentum with the passage of time.

**NOTES & REFERENCES**


1. W.W. Hunter, *The Imperial Gazetteer of India,* Vol. XXIII, Oxford, 1908, p. 1.
2. F.B. Bradley Birt, *Chotanagpur, A Litte-Known Province of the Empire,* London, 1910, p. 85.
3. A.D. Tuckey, *Final Report on the Resettlement of the Kolhan Government Estate in the District of Singhbhum 1913-1918,* Patna, 1920, p. 17.
4. Mathew Areeparampil, 'Migration of the Hos to Singhbhum' in A.K. Sen (ed) *Singhbhum: Some Historical Gleanings, Chaibasa,* 1986, pp. 14-15.
5. Murali Sahu, *The Kolhan under the British Rule,* Calcutta, 1985, p. 77.
6. Letter from J. Reid to the Commissioner of the Chotanagpur Division, Ranchi, N. 5333 of 2 September, 1914, *vide* Record of Rights of Mankis and Mundas for use in the Kolhan Government Estate, Fly Leaf of Deputy Commissioner, Singhbhum Revenue Department, Collection No. III Settlement, File No. 20-7-6 of 1914, District Record Room, Chaibasa.
7. M. Areeparampil, *Struggle for Swaraj, A History of Adivasi Movements in Jharkhand,* Chaibasa, 2000, pp. 6-7.
8. D.N. Majumdar, *The Affairs of a Tribe,* Lucknow, 1950, p. 256.
9. *Ibid.,* p. 257.
10. M. Areeparampil, 'Forest Andolan in Singhbhum', in S. Narayan (ed.), *Jharkhand Movements: Origin and Evolution,* Inter-India Publication, New Delhi, p. 149.
11. J.A. Craven, *Final Report on the Settlement of the Kolhan Government Estate,* Singhbhum, 1897, Calcutta, 1898, p. 41.
12. Tucky, Final Report, p. 38.
13. Letter from Wilkinson to R.D. Mangles, N 12 of 11 October 1836, Summary of events from 1805-1836 and origin of taking over by government of the four Kol Pirs of Aula, Lalgarh, Bantaria and Thai from Mayurbhanj, DC's office, Judicial Department, CN XII, FN XII 7 of 1930, D.R.R. Chaibasa.
14. Letter from W. Grey to W.S. Seton-Karr, Spare Copies of P.I. Porahat papers from 1857 to 1862, No. 31 of 29 December, 1857, Bihar State Archives, Patna.
15. P.C. Roychaudhary, *Bihar District Gazetteers,* Singhbhum, Patna, 1958, p. 109.

16. A.K. Sen 'Protected Forest Rules and Ho Social Protest' in C.K. Paty (Ed), *Forest, Government and Tribe,* New Delhi, 2006, pp. 80-81.
17. O.P. Kishore and Anubhav Malhotra, *Forest Manual (Bihar and Jharkhand),* Patna, 2006, p. 1.
18. *Ibid.,* Part II, pp. 1-3.
19. *Ibid.,* Appendix 1, pp. 1-2.
20. *Ibid.,* Part III, p. 53.
21. Govind Mukhuiti, *Van Ki Ladai,* People's Union for Democratic Rights, New Delhi, April 1982, pp. 19-20.
22. *Singhbhum Ekta Saptahik,* Chaibasa, August 1978, second issue, p. 4.
23. Areeparampil, *Forest Andolan,* pp. 152-53.
24. *Ulgulan* (Jharkhand Mukti-Morcha Ka Mukhpatra), 1-15 September, 1983, p. 5.
25. *Singhbhum Ekta,* October 1978, second issue, p. 1.
26. *Ibid.,* December, 1979, first issue, p. 4.
27. C.K. Paty, 'Jungle Katai Andolan (1978) and Singhbhum' in Paty (Ed), *Forest Government and Tribe,* p. 96.
28. *Repression in Singhbhum,* report of the Fact Finding Committee of the People's Union for Civil Liberties and Democratic Rights, Delhi in Bihar, March 1979, p. 1.
29. *Singhbhum Ekta,* September 1980, second issue, p. 2.
30. *Hashiye ki Aawaj,* Social Action Trust, New Delhi, June 2007, p. 4.
31. *Singhbhum Ekta,* September, 1982, first issue, p. 6.
32. Areeparampil, *Jungle Aur Adivasi : Shoshan Ke Shikar,* Tribal Research and Training Centre, Chaibasa, 1988, pp. I-II.
33. Paty, *Jungle Katai Andolan,* p. 98.
34. Balbir Dutt, *Kahani Jharkhand Andolan Ki,* Crown Publication, Ranchi, 2005, p. 462.
35. *Adivasi Ashtitva ke Liye Vishal Rally,* Handbill of Macha Kumuti, published by Ramesh Jerai, Johar, Chaibasa.
36. Memorandum of Macha Kumuti (Co-Ordination of Public Organisations) dated 10.11.2005, Adivasi Club Bhawan, Harigutu, Madkamhatu, Chaibasa, West Singhbhum.
37. *Dainik Jagran,* Jamshedpur, 9 December 2007.
38. *Prabhat Khabar,* Jamshedpur, 25 December, 2007.

# Index